NORTH EASTERN MOTORSPORT

A CENTURY OF MEMORIES

LARRY CARTER

AMBERLEY

First published 2022

Amberley Publishing
The Hill, Stroud,
Gloucestershire, GL5 4EP

www.amberley-books.com

ISBN: 978 1 3981 1172 1 (print)
ISBN: 978 1 3981 1173 8 (ebook)

British Library Cataloguing in Publication Data.
A catalogue record for this book is available from the British Library.

Typeset in 10pt on 13pt Celeste.
Typesetting by SJmagic DESIGN SERVICES, India.
Printed in the UK.

CONTENTS

FOREWORD

They say there's a first time for everything and in among a varied and fulfilled life, in my eightieth year, I've been asked to write my first foreword to a book.

I'm not sure what I'm supposed to write other than what wonderful memories I have of racing cars in the carefree days of the 1960s and 1970s at race circuits all over the country, including here in the North East, many of which are sadly no longer.

When I started out in scrambling, my father quickly realised that I'd be much safer on four wheels than two, so my career went in that direction after that and some of my fondest and early recollections are racing my Morris Minor at places like Ouston, Ingliston, Rufforth and, of course, Croft.

Being a Geordie, we had many tracks on our doorstep back then, which helped as I was busy running a garage with my brother, so it meant we didn't have to spend lots of time travelling, unless it was much further afield, of course, and then it was quite a trip from Newcastle.

Little did we know at the time as we were just young lads having fun, but some of those races in the 1,000 cc Special Saloon class became the stuff of legends, as depicted later in these pages.

I, and the likes of Ken Walker and Sedric Bell, all had highly tuned Minis in which we used to do battle, and then along came Alex Clacher in his Imp to add to proceedings. We used to fight like sworn enemies on track but afterwards, whoever had won, we celebrated in the Croft clubhouse until it was time to leave. We all lived relatively locally, so getting home was never a problem.

Occasionally, we got paired with the bigger-capacity cars and I recall it was a little daunting when my Mini was up against the Chevrolet Camaros, Ford Boss Mustangs and Ford Falcons, which dwarfed it. But I always gave them a good run for their money!

I'm told I won sixty-eight races around Croft, which is a fantastic achievement and each one was special, whether in my Morris Minor or latterly in the Formula Libre March. There were a couple of big accidents too, one where I nearly lost my arm, but generally speaking, we had a wonderful time.

I even bought myself a trials bike when I'd finished racing, so I suppose I'm as qualified as anyone to write a few words about most disciplines in the book.

The North East has provided many successful competitors and iconic venues over the last century and I'm delighted that some of them are recorded for posterity in these pages. It's certainly jogged a few memories for me and it's a shame that some of us, like Sedric and Alex for example, are no longer around to reminisce about the good old days over a pint or two in the clubhouse.

I'm blessed to have achieved the success I've had over the years, and it's been a privilege to have been asked to contribute these words to what is an iconic and nostalgic look back at the wonderful world of motorsport from our region.

I hope you enjoy reading this book as much as I enjoyed making some of the memories.

Andy Barton

Andy Barton. (Andy Ellis)

GUARDS INTERNATIONAL TROPHY MEETING – CROFT 1970: FUTURE FORMULA ONE STARS DESCEND ON CROFT

The summer of 1970 will be remembered for many things: the pivotal beginning of a new decade, the age of flower power, the Isle of Wight festival and that save of the century from Gordon Banks in the World Cup in Mexico, although his heroics couldn't stop the world champions, England, going out.

It was a significant day too in local motor racing circles as on Saturday 11 July 1970 it was the superstars of tomorrow who descended on Croft. The British Formula Three Championship was the proving ground for future world champions at the time and with the Guards International Trophy Meeting incorporating a round, it was to be one of the highest-profile meetings ever to be held in the region.

Future stars competing at Croft that day included future world champions Niki Lauda and James Hunt, brilliant Brazilians Carlos Pace and Wilson Fittipaldi, and a host of home-grown and international stars in the fifty-car field necessitating two heats.

Pace, in his privately entered Lotus, won the opening heat ahead of Swede Freddy Kottulinsky (Liptons Racing Division Lotus) and Swiss Jurg Dubler (Chevron). Heat two saw Aussie Dave Walker victorious in his Gold Leaf Team Lotus ahead of Gerry Birrell's Brabham and Mike Beuttler's similar car in third to set up a fantastic final.

Thirty laps of intense racing around Croft's 1.75-mile perimeter circuit lay ahead and it was Walker who led the field, but he clattered the infamous Chicane on lap one and was out. It left Pace to come through the pack to take the win ahead of Dubler with Beuttler in third. Fourth went to Gerry Birrell, with fellow Brabham driver Tony Trimmer in fifth while sixth was Wilson Fittipaldi, elder brother of Emerson who went on to win the 1972 and 1974 Formula One titles. James Hunt finished ninth.

Helmut Kelleners' 7,600 cc striking-red March 707 Chevrolet CanAm was a sight to behold that day too, the mighty machine just fitting through the chicane, with Chris Craft charging behind in his McLaren for the Jock Leith Trophy. It all came to a spectacular end when Craft clipped the tyre markers at the Esses, ripping the front bodywork off the car leaving the German to win easily.

The battle of the Group Two Saloons was a spectacle in its own right too, as Australian Frank Gardner wrestled his awesome 5-litre Ford Boss Mustang to a double victory in the Glover

Trophy Race ahead of fellow countryman Brian Muir in his Chevrolet Camaro. It concluded an unforgettable day with the best entry at Croft since the WD and HO Wills Trophy Meeting four years previously, which included the likes of Bruce McLaren, Denny Hulme, Chris Amon, John Surtees, Brian Redman, Peter Gethin, Innes Ireland and David Hobbs.

That meeting took place in the summer of 1966, and I cannot for the life of me think what other memorable sporting moment occurred back then, only this time it was 4-2 in England's favour over West Germany. They think it's all over and all that...

Left: The programme cover from the 1970 meeting. (Terry Wright)

Below: Formula Three cars thunder underneath the famous Croft footbridge. (Tony Todd)

Dave Walker negotiates the
Chicane. (Tony Todd)

Graham Birrell's Ford Escort Twin Cam on the grass paddock. (Tony Todd)

Dennis Leech leads Frank Gardner in their respective Ford Boss Mustangs. (Tony Todd)

SCOTT TRIAL GOLDEN JUBILEE: YORKSHIRE GRIT AS WILKINSON WINS

When it comes to one of the greatest sporting events in the country, yet one of the least well known, the Scott Trial has a heritage steeped in history for over 100 years.

Apart from a short foray over the border to what is now Cleveland, it's been a Yorkshire institution inaugurated by Alfred Scott and his select gathering of disciples back in 1914.

Two world wars notwithstanding, the toughest one-day trial in the world headed for its 50th anniversary in 1964, and what an event it turned out to be.

Yorkshiremen have dominated the 'Scott' over the years, with names such as Lampkin, Jefferies, Langton and Nicholson having all landed the prestigious trophy prior to the Golden Jubilee version, which took place on Saturday 31 October 1964. This trial is scary enough without any reminders with it being held on Halloween!

The significance of the fiftieth running might have been coincidental as to most competitors, it was just another Scott they wanted to win. But at least the weather was playing ball, as this particular year it was so dry even some villages on the moors were rationing water, but while the rivers and streams may have been shallower than normal, as one competitor quipped, 'The rocks don't evaporate!'

As ever a quality field of 165 riders had been assembled to tackle the 64-mile course containing fifty-nine sections around Swaledale, with many of those tests used then still featuring in the modern-day format. Back then, huge crowds made their way to popular sections such as Orgate Falls, Bridge End, Whaw Bridge and the now sadly absent Washfold Splash where one of the attractions in the tiny hamlet of Hurst was the Green Dragon pub, which always did a roaring trade on Scott days. If ever you are up that way, the property is now a house, but it still retains the sign on the gable end.

Winning the Scott verges on being parochially swayed to keeping the Alfred Scott Memorial Trophy within the boundaries of Britian's largest county and while Yorkshire doesn't have any physical borders, you'd think it had. When a Yorkshireman didn't win, it didn't sit well in the noggin-and-natter evenings at clubhouses around the region for the next year.

So, imagine the delight when a twenty-three-year-old from Kettlewell by the name of William Wilkinson emerged up the field from where he had started some 4 hours, 8 minutes, and 34 seconds earlier aboard his trusty 246 cc factory-supported Greeves, to set

Standard Time. William, or Bill to everyone who knew him, and his younger brother Mick were regulars on the local off-road scene and popular among their fellow competitors, so it would be a long wait until the tallies on the observation cards were totted up.

Irishman Sammy Miller had taken victory on three previous occasions, including the past two years, and despite a bout of flu he had sacrificed a little time to make sure he was best on observation. And he was, but the six marks lost on time was to prove crucial and when the results were announced later that evening it was Wilkinson who was crowned the winner by just three marks.

Indeed, bettering the legend that was Miller, who would go on to claim another four victories in the following years, was cause for celebration as Bill had seen off the likes of Ray Sayer, Jim Sandiford, motocross aces Jeff Smith and John Banks, as well as Arthur and Alan Lampkin to name a few of the ninety-one finishers.

It turned out to be Wilkinson's one and only Scott victory and the only one also for erstwhile British manufacturer Greeves, with whom Bill had a long and successful career, before the impending success of Spanish motorcycles such as Bultaco and Montesa over the next fifteen years.

It proved to be an omen too as for the next couple of decades, Yorkshiremen dominated the Scott with only a handful of interlopers such as Miller, Cumbrian Nigel Birkett and Clevelander Rob Edwards, very nearly a Yorkshireman, claiming the winner's trophy.

The 1964 programme cover featuring Sammy Miller, who won the previous year. (Cartersport)

Above left: Winner Bill Wilkinson negotiates the Bridge End section on his 250 cc Greeves. (Mortons Archive)

Above right: J. Addyman (BSA – 95) and D. Robinson (Greeves – 70) come to grief at Bridge End. (Mortons Archive)

Left: A. J. Davis shows the crowd how to do it on his Greeves. (Mortons Archive)

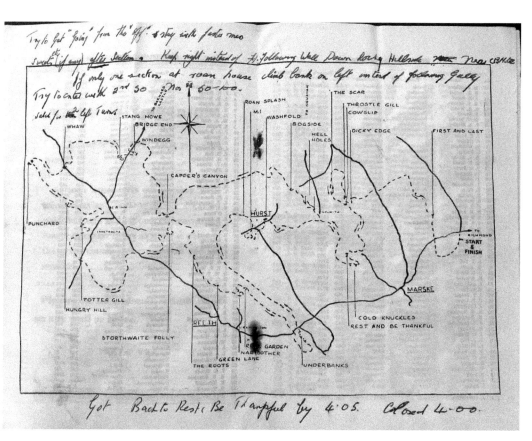

The 1964 route with notes for future made by a competitor, Leslie Wade, erroneously listed as 'J. Wade' in the entry list. (Cartersport)

13

SCOTT TRIAL COMES HOME: KING GERALD THE FIRST

Head up to Swaledale and Arkengarthdale and engage the locals in conversation; I guarantee it won't be long before the subject gets around to the Scott Trial. It's part of the heritage up there, but the world's toughest one-day time and observation trial hasn't always been held around the hamlets of Marske, Hurst, Fremington, Langthwaite and Whaw, as well as the tourist Mecca of Reeth.

The event began in 1914 when Alfred Scott, inventor and founder of the Scott Motorcycle Company, challenged the workers at his factory to ride from the factory in Shipley through the Yorkshire Dales. Of the fourteen starters, only nine finished. The event was reintroduced after the First World War in 1919 and although Alfred Scott died in 1923, the event continued to be run by the Scott workers until 1926.

Bradford and District Motor Club took over and held 'the Scott' around Blubberhouses until 1938 when the permission to use the land was withdrawn, meaning that a new home at Swainby was found for the immediate years after the Second World War. A reorganisation of boundaries by the sport's governing body in 1950 saw a switch to Swaledale under the auspices of Darlington and District Motor Club until 1990 when current custodians Richmond and District Motor Club took over and continue to put on a wonderful event annually. Well, that was until something called Covid appeared in 2020 and we all know what happened then.

While it has been the domain of plenty of Yorkshiremen over the years, one in particular has made an indelible mark on the event. Gerald Richardson, who lives only half a dozen miles from the start, set a number of records during his tenure, some that stand to this day, including two fantastic wins in 1983 and 1985.

One of four competing brothers from Skeeby, this Richardson contested his first Scott Trial in 1980, learning the skill and survival techniques needed to not only get round the 70-mile, eighty-section moorland course of bogs, streams, rocks, and everything else mother nature could throw at it, but to beat 200 other competitors.

By 1983, he was established sufficiently to give his fourth attempt a proper go, but things didn't go to plan due to a last-minute change of machinery. Having ridden his Gatenby Italjet on the weekend previous' Red Rose Trial, the frame had broken and due to difficulty obtaining parts the week before the Scott, it looked as if he'd have to sit it out. But with the help of mechanic Tim Bell and importer Nick Jefferies, a new British-built Armstrong machine was secured on the Friday evening before the trial started on the following Saturday morning. Talk about cutting it fine!

However, the day couldn't have gone much better, and Gerald had a strong ride without any major problems to set fastest time and with third best marks on observation, he claimed a sensational win. Some, however, were a little less than gracious and suggested it was all too good to be true and there'd been some cheating going on. But there hadn't and as a result, Richardson became the very first winner from the Richmond area to lift the Alfred Scott Memorial Trophy for the first time and he'd done it on a bike he'd only seen for the first time, let alone ridden, the day before.

The victory heralded the first win on the Scott for a British machine since Arthur Lampkin won on a BSA in 1965, and no one has taken victory on a British bike since, so that makes it another two notches on the belt!

If winning in 1983 was hard, trying to defend his crown proved tougher and Gerald narrowly lost out in 1984. Some confusion over the section markers in the final part of the event around Goats Splash near Helwith saw him 'five' both back-to-back sections (called 'subs') meaning he had to settle for second place.

He wasn't in any mood to finish second in 1985, however, and aboard a Yamaha, scorched round the moors in an incredible time of 4 hours, 15 minutes and 45 seconds which, despite the course varying from year to year, is still the benchmark 'Standard Time' today as no one has gone quicker in the past thirty-five years. He was second best on observation to win by the two marks, which significantly, he'd lost out to the year previous.

Injury hampered his 1986 attempt having broken his wrist on the run up, and with no training it proved too tough even for a gritty Yorkshireman. Despite setting Standard Time on a couple more occasions, and challenging for the hat-trick, sadly Gerald couldn't quite manage that elusive third win and eventually called it a day in 2003.

As well as the two wins, Richardson won a total of seven gold and seven silver coveted Scott Spoons (first-class awards) and remarkably finished nineteen events on the trot without retiring. That in itself is bordering on yet another record to add to the rest.

It doesn't end there, though, as in the history spanning over a century of this great event, while tipping a nod in the direction of four-times winner Philip Alderson from Askrigg, only one other rider from Richmondshire has won the Scott since, and that was a certain Jonathan Richardson who took a sensational victory in 2011.

By doing so, 'Jono' joined his dad to become only the second father and son to win this prestigious event alongside Martin Lampkin and his son Dougie, who is now a twelve-times world champion. Anyone who knows Gerald can vouch he's not one to dish out compliments easily, but on this occasion he's both happy and proud that his lad won on his third attempt whereas it took himself four cracks before he took a win.

Making sure she doesn't get left out of the limelight, daughter Chloe is one of an increasing number of ladies who tackle this daunting event these days. Since making her debut in 2012, she has been classed as a finisher most years and if determination counts for anything, she's every bit as good as her dad and her brother.

Above: Richardson tackles the Surrender section in 1987, two years after his last win. (Neil Sturgeon)

Left: And the same section a year later with an equally large group of onlookers. (Neil Sturgeon)

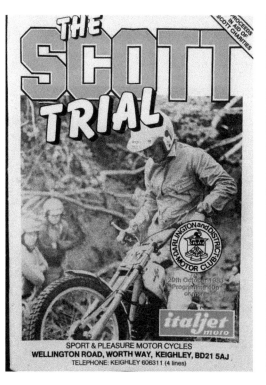

The programme covers from Gerald Richardson's two Scott Trial victories. (Cartersport)

Scott Trial winners, father and son. Gerald congratulates Jonathan at the finish. (Neil Sturgeon)

EUROPE'S BEST TAKE ON THE HOME GUARD: RENNISON AND SHIELD COME OF AGE

Often classed as motorsport's best-kept secret, the sport of Rallycross is the youngest of all powered disciplines, with a history going back just over fifty years.

Popular myth always had it that back in November 1967, the world's leading rally competitors had assembled for the RAC Rally only for it to be cancelled at the last minute due to the foot and mouth outbreak that year. With a television schedule to fill, a hastily planned meeting was arranged at Lydden Hill in Kent for drivers to compete in a bio-secure environment and thus the sport was born.

Not so, as it already existed having been invented in February of that year. With television revolutionising people's lives and sporting outside broadcasts gaining in popularity, regional production company ABC Television commissioned a number of specially invited rally drivers to race on a part-gravel, part-asphalt track at Lydden to be broadcast by ITV as part of their new flagship *World of Sport* show.

That test event was won by Vic Elford in a Porsche, who was later to become a Formula One driver and winner of the 1968 Monte Carlo Rally, and such was the success that the TV bosses commissioned a series of events split between Lydden Hill (near Dover) and Croft Autodrome in the north.

The ITV World of Sport Rallycross Championship ran for a couple of years before the BBC wanted a slice of the action for their rival Saturday afternoon sporting talismanic *Grandstand* show and over the next few years, as the television companies battled for viewing figures mainly over winter, so too did the drivers who rapidly became household names.

Rally legend, Roger Clark and his brother Stan, Peter Harper, Barry Lee, Pip Carrotte and 'Jumping' Jeff Williamson were just some of the names to grace the grid in the early days whereby such was the fledgling nature of the circuits combined with the worst of the British winter, cars often got stuck in the mud and driver visibility led to a number of spectacular crashes. Sadly, very little television footage exists these days as, with the broadcasts going out live at the time, nothing was recorded for posterity.

Unlike Lydden, Croft's original layout was anti-clockwise and featured a combination of asphalt on the racetrack, grass and mud on the infield and broken dolomite from the old runways and service roads. One such meeting was just after Christmas in 1968 when the ITV cameras turned up to show a round of the *World of Sport* series.

Rallycross lasted into the early 1970s at Croft with international competitors regularly visiting including the Dutch de Rooy brothers, Jan and Harry, in their all-conquering bright orange four-wheel drive, variomatic DAFs powered by a Renault Gordini engine. The sport gradually faded from popularity and when the gates closed for the final time in 1981, that looked to be the end of the road for Croft hosting this spectacular sport.

Conversely, the very nature of the sport running on rough or loose surfaces meant it was ideal for the decaying asphalt, which meant circuit racing was no longer viable and, with planning permits still in place, local businessman George Shield formed a consortium to run Rallycross. In 1982, they set about building a track using the existing circuit layout in a clockwise direction and with lots of local support from fans and drivers alike, a new era was born.

The proximity of the circuit gave rise to many local competitors and as the decade progressed, Rallycross allowed a sanctuary for the fire-breathing Group B Supercars that were outlawed from rallying following a number of bad accidents. The boom-and-bust 1980s meant plenty of extravagance and soon grids were packed to overflowing in the various British championships that were held at Croft.

All of that success, combined with one of the fastest tracks in Europe, saw the prestigious Inter Nations Cup awarded to the North East track, and in November 1987 virtually all of Europe's best drivers descended on North Yorkshire for the team event involving eight countries. Included in the British team were two young lads from Darlington: Mark Rennison, in his DSRM-supported Ford RS200, and near neighbour from Cleasby, Michael Shield, son of the circuit operator, in his MG Metro 6R4.

In front of 15,000 fans on a gloomy winter Saturday, Team GB won the opening two heats with Will Gollop and John Welch taking victory after Rennison's car had suffered engine problems in qualifying. The home team extended their lead following Trevor Hopkins' win while Michael Shield had to give second best to Finnish driver Seppo Nittymaki later in the day to ensure Great Britain held the lead overnight.

Shield won the opening heat on Sunday before Rennison, whose crew had worked through the night to replace the engine with one which was some 200 bhp less, won also with Gollop again victorious to extend the British lead. The Europeans battled back into contention despite another win for 'Renny' in the final set of heats as the all-important finals beckoned.

Swede Ollie Arnesson won the 'E' Final in his Audi Quattro with Shield in third while the 'D' Final went the way of Finland's Matti Alamaki (Lancia Delta) with Welch (Opel Xtrac) second. London-based Cypriot Dimi Mavropoulos won the 'C' Final for GB in his Audi before Gollop scorched to victory in the 'B' Final in his MG Metro 6R4.

That meant that all Rennison had to do was finish the 'A' Final to clinch the crown for Great Britain, who had finished third and second in the two previous INC events, and he did just that, finishing second to Seppo Nittymaki's Peugeot 205 T16. The end result saw Great Britain finish on 159 points ahead of Finland on 148 and Sweden on 135 whereby many claimed it was the best rallycross meeting ever, not only at Croft, but in the UK.

Rallycross continued at Croft for another two decades, even hosting the British Grand Prix on a number of occasions. But despite its heritage from the very start, rallycross no longer features on the schedule at Croft and although venues such as Langbaurgh in Middlesbrough and Tockwith near Wetherby hosted the odd rallycross event in the recent past, for the first time in half a century the region is devoid of the sport.

Above: Local lad Mark Rennison helped the British team to victory despite problems. (Tony Todd)

Left: John Welch in his Astra, which he also took to a win. (Tony Todd)

An unusual aerial shot of the Croft rallycross track showing the venue packed to capacity for the Inter Nations Cup meeting. (Tony Todd)

Above: Local driver John Cockerill in rallycross action at Croft in the early 1970s with very much a rally-prepared Ford Escort. (Tony Todd)

Right: The programme cover for the Inter Nations Cup event in 1987. (Cartersport)

MAC HOBSON: THE FASTEST GEORDIE ON THREE WHEELS

With Tyneside traditionally being a hotbed of motorcycle racing, and with a copious amount of sidecar racers falling into that bracket over the years, the fact that Mac Hobson was revered as the best of them all was some accolade indeed.

Born Malcolm Hobson on 7 June 1931 in Gosforth, it wasn't a case of success coming late to the Geordie dubbed 'Mac', it just wasn't really noticed in the early days. Originally a solo racer where he started his career in the early 1950s, making his debut at the Manx Grand Prix in 1958 before going on to contest the Junior TT in 1962 aboard an AJS where he lapped at 82.80 mph on his way to forty-first place.

Mac bettered that the following year by taking a twentieth position in the same race before the sidecar bug bit and he took a Norton to twenty-first place in the Sidecar TT of 1964. And from that point in time, he never looked back as he gradually became one of Britain's (and latterly the world's) greatest sidecar racing exponents.

His mild-mannered persona coupled with his bespectacled appearance belied the fact that Hobson was a different animal on track, given the way he ferociously drove his various outfits. His career was initially cut short just as it was taking off following an accident at Darley Moor in 1972, which cost the life of his passenger John Hartridge who was also a personal friend, near neighbour and work colleague.

As a result, Hobson retired from the sport he loved but that passion never left him, and he was often seen on the gate at North East Motor Cycle Racing Club meetings at Croft collecting admission money or enjoying a drink on the club nights, but he cut a forlorn and lonely figure, and it was inevitable he would get back to competing again.

So, in 1974, he'd exorcised enough demons to return to competition and despite his self-enforced absence he'd lost none of his flair, talent or indeed speed as he won the British Sidecar Championship at his first attempt. He retained his title the following season and that same year – 1975 – he scored his first Isle of Man TT podium when he finished second in the 500 cc Sidecar TT aboard a Yamaha, recording a speed of 95.85 mph in the process.

It was only a matter of time before that first TT win came and Hobson topped the podium for the first time in 1976 before adding a second TT victory in 1977. Success was now transpiring on the world stage also, with Hobson and passenger Stu Collins scoring points in the Dutch, Belgian and Czechoslovakian Grands Prix that year too, which proved to be a significant one in motorcycle sport as not only did Barry Sheene retain the 500 cc World Championship, but George O'Dell, and passengers Kenny Arthur and Cliff Holland, became the first Brits to land the World Sidecar Championship since Eric Oliver in 1953.

At the age of forty-six, Hobson was now ready for a full tilt at the World Championship in 1978 and teamed up with the studious passenger Kenny Birch aboard the now-legendary Seymaz-chassised Hamilton Yamaha, dubbed the Ham-Yam and depicted by a cartoon pig on the fairing.

However, sidecar racing was about to go through a major transformation thanks to innovative Swiss engineer Rolf Biland interpreting the rule books to good effect and building an outfit like no one had seen before. The Beo-Imagine device was basically a racing car on three wheels where the passenger, in this case Kenny Williams, just sat in the integral pod, without having to perform the balance acrobatics of his rivals.

Many deemed it unfair, and indeed it would only last a season before the rules were redefined, but Biland and the Beo were to prove a nemesis for Hobson that season. Mac led the opening Grand Prix in Austria only to end up second behind Biland, then a week later at Nogaro in France, Biland cleared off again leaving Hobson to come home third, but still held joint second place in the standings.

Problems ensued with a non-score at the next round in Italy, but Hobson was still in with a shout. While back home, he led the British championship after winning three of the opening four rounds as they headed over to the Isle of Man for the 1978 TT. The island was abuzz with the return of Mike Hailwood after eleven years away and the vast crowd was still soaking up the legend's win in Saturday's TT Formula One when Monday's opening sidecar race came about.

There had been some consternation about a bump that had been allegedly caused by some roadworks on Bray Hill just a few hundred metres from the start, and it was something of concern for the low-slung outfits, which one journalist described as 'glass fibre carpet slippers' and Biland's Beo in particular 'resembling a cross between a bumper car and a rocket ship'.

As the field streamed away in pairs led by Bill Hodgkins/John Parkins and Mick Boddice/Chas Birks, Hobson and Birch readied themselves somewhat uneasily. Graham Milton/John Brushwood and Steve Sinnott/Clive Pocklington set off next. Biland and Williams were paired with Hobson and Birch and the foursome screamed away from the line with Biland's futuristic projectile ahead of Hobson's more conventional unit.

Then the unthinkable happened as Hobson and Birch gave chase: their outfit hit the raised cover, which had caused some concern prior to the race, and at around 100 mph flipped it over. Both driver and passenger were killed instantly in the horrific crash as they descended Bray Hill, but the tragedy wasn't over as Swiss champion Ernst Trachsel hit the debris and joined Mac and Kenny on the TT tragedy list.

Oblivious to what had gone on, Biland continued, but his race came to an abrupt end with a mechanical failure, which eventual winner Dick Greasley narrowly avoided clattering into the back of, while future British world champion Jock Taylor, later to lose his own life in a racing accident, claimed second place.

Hearing of the tragedy befalling his friend and rival afterwards, Biland headed back home to Switzerland immediately and didn't take part in the second race later in the week. Britain, and in particular Tyneside, had lost one of their favourite sons in a tragedy that many people felt should not have happened.

Above left: The bespectacled Mac Hobson pictured in 1968. (Mortons Archive)

Above right: With Mick Burns as passenger and backing from Hamilton Motorcycles, Hobson negotiates the Croft Chicane. (Tony Todd)

Mac Hobson and Kenny Birch (6) set off alongside Rolf Biland and Kenny Williams (5) at the start of the fateful 1978 Sidecar TT race. (Nick Nicholls Collection at Mortons Archive)

Above: Just a couple of weeks before their accident, Mac and Kenny were in action in the British Championship, seen here at Brands Hatch. (Nick Nicholls Collection at Mortons Archive)

Right: Mac Hobson adorns the cover of the 1976 British Championship meeting at Croft. (Cartersport)

BRITISH CHAMPIONSHIP ROAD RACES CROFT AUTODROME

SATURDAY 19th JUNE 1976

Determination in every line British Sidecar Champion Mac Hobson.

OFFICIAL PROGRAMME
20p

RACING 50 MOTOR CYCLE CLUB

KEN REDFERN: THE GENTLEMAN RACER

Certain memories stay with you, indelibly etched for life, and such a one for me was sitting, aged ten, in the windswept and decidedly damp (and long since gone) grandstand at Croft Autodrome when the PA crackled into life to announce that Ken Redfern, the quiet and unassuming local motorcycle racing hero, who had taken on and regularly beaten the best in the world, had been killed.

I'll admit I was too young to know of Ken's exploits on his home-prepared 750 cc Norton Domiracer where on consecutive weekends back in 1969, at Cadwell Park and Mallory Park, he had finished second to the Italian megastar Giacomo Agostini on the works MV Agusta. Cheered on by crowds in excess of 50,000 at both venues, one of the famous names Redfern beat at Mallory Park was a certain Mike Hailwood.

Originally from Stockton before moving to Hutton Rudby, Ken, and latterly his brother Mike, made his debut at Croft on a Manx Norton and quickly became the man to beat. His first major victory came at Snetterton, however, as he climbed the ladder from clubman to established star in a relatively short period of time.

He progressed from the 350 cc and 500 cc Nortons to a 350 cc Aermacchi and then onto the 750 cc Norton, scoring considerable success at meetings around the country. One such result came at the famous 1971 Race of the Year at Mallory Park when he enjoyed a race-long battle in the MCN Superbike race to claim third behind works stars Ray Pickrell and Percy Tait.

Following those races, Ken went on to ride for London-based team owners Paul Dunstall and Gus Kuhn, continually perfecting and developing the bikes, but his life was cut tragically short when he was involved in a freak road accident on Saturday 30 June 1973 between Yarm and Kirklevington, not far from where the entrance to Judges Hotel is now.

Just about every year since his accident, the perpetual 'Ken Redfern Trophy' has been fiercely contested by the sport's leading lights. Held at venues such as Croft, Oliver's Mount, Scarborough and East Fortune, names who have landed the trophy over the years include everyone's favourite television biker Guy Martin, local Guisborough ace Dennis Hobbs, as well as TT legends Joey Dunlop and John McGuinness among many others. They are all on the famous Flying Geese cup, which replicates Redfern's unique helmet design.

One such meeting took place at Croft in September 1975 with the North East Motor Cycle Racing Club hosting a national road race meeting for the Ken Redfern Trophy. As ever there was a star-studded field to contest the various races including future double world champion Kork Ballington from South Africa. A fledgling twenty-one-year-old, Ron Haslam was there along with other national stars Steve Manship, Roger Marshall, and Scot Bill Simpson.

Ballington kicked things off with a win in the 250 cc race on his Yamaha ahead of local hero Alan Stewart (PA Yamaha) with Mac Hobson, and passenger Gordon Russell (700 cc Ham-Yam), taking the first sidecar race. Manship edged out Ballington to win the ten-lap 350 cc race on his Manchester Yamaha with Haslam third before Shildon's Ray Bell/Terry Bradley (Konig) won the second sidecar race.

Manship won the 500 cc race ahead of Haslam and Paul Cott before the gladiators lined up for the feature race for the Ken Redfern Trophy over fifteen laps. As expected, the leading lights scrapped it out with the lap record smashed on a number of occasions. Ballington, Haslam and Manship all took it in turns to lead before the latter two succumbed to the pressure and left the South African to pick up the prestigious trophy on his 350 cc Yamaha.

The late and well-respected photographer Spencer Oliver paid tribute in the programme by saying: 'In my association with motorsport, stretching back over half a century, I have seldom met anyone more fitted to the title of "Gentleman" than Ken Redfern and for those that knew him, his passing has left a void which will never be filled.'

In recent times, there have been calls for a section of track at Croft to be renamed in Ken's honour. How fitting that would be if it came to pass that one of the North East's best motorcycle racers could be immortalised in such an appropriate manner?

Above: A rare colour picture of Ken in action at Mallory Park on the 750 cc Dunstall Dominator. (Mortons Archive)

Right: Ken Redfern (centre) with close friends Keith Jeal (left) and Stewart Hodgson (right). (Mortons Archive)

Left: Exiting Mountside Hairpin at Oliver's Mount, Scarborough, with the famous 'Flying Geese' crash helmet prominent. (Mortons Archive)

Below: Redfern's smooth and efficient style is put to good effect at the Croft Chicane. (Mortons Archive)

OFFICIAL PROGRAMME - 20p

NORTH EAST MOTOR CYCLE RACING CLUB

CROFT AUTODROME,
Near Darlington

NATIONAL ROAD RACE MEETING

KEN REDFERN TROPHY

SATURDAY, 20th SEPT., 1975

AT 1.00 p.m.

ADMISSION CHARGE 80p

Permit No. 933

Printed by J. Holmes Ltd., 4 Byker Bridge, Newcastle upon Tyne, 1

The programme cover for the 1975 Ken Redfern Trophy meeting at Croft Autodrome won by future world champion Kork Ballington. (Cartersport)

BATTLE OF BRITAIN MEETINGS: REMEMBERING THE FEW

While one of the most important battles of the Second World War, and in British history, was mainly played out in the skies some 300 miles south as the RAF fended off the Luftwaffe in the Battle of Britain, the lasting testament to 'The Few' became one of the most successful meetings in the history of Croft Autodrome.

One common misnomer is that RAF Croft (originally RAF Dalton-on-Tees) played a significant role in the Battle of Britain, hence the commemoration of the meetings bearing the name when in fact the airfield only became operational in 1941, just as that part of the conflict was ending.

Croft, however, did become a strategic part in the war effort as the first squadron to join the airfield was No. 78 Squadron RAF, which arrived on 20 October 1941 before leaving in June 1942. Later that year, the Royal Canadian Air Force arrived, and their various squadrons remained until the end of hostilities in 1945.

The Battle of Britain race meetings started at Thornaby Airfield in 1960 as a celebration, and fund raiser, for the Royal Air Forces Association and organised by Darlington and District Motor Club (D&DMC). That first event included Brian Redman in a Mini who went on to be a professional racing driver in Sports Cars and also included a stint in the Ferrari works Formula One team. He also raced in Formula Two, Can Am and notably Formula 5,000, the latter two in America.

It also included Tony Lanfranchi (Austin Healey and Frazer Nash), Campbell Dawson of Willow Bridge Service Station near Scotch Corner, Darlington's only Formula One driver to date, Jimmy Blumer (Cooper Monaco), Jill Hutchinson (Bristol Special), Keith Schellenberg (Barnato Hassan Bentley) and Bruce Ropner (Napier) who both went on to found Croft Autodrome.

In 1961 the Battle of Britain moved to Catterick Airfield before moving to its spiritual home of Croft in 1965 where the event consisted of a combination of cars, bikes, and sidecars for the first time, with fifty-two cars, 102 solos and thirty-eight 'three-wheelers'. D&DMC was unique in being able to run mixed events as it was members of both the MSA, which governed car racing, and the ACU, which governed motorcycle sport.

By now an aerial display was included and in 1966 the Red Arrows opened the event. In 1967 the sidecars featured Colin Appleyard, Mac Hobson and Ray Bell, which provided great entertainment for the sizeable crowd. The entry fee for cars was £3 3s with substantial prize money being £12 for first place down to £4 for fourth, while the class winners received £8.

By 1973 the Battle of Britain meeting was well established in the calendar and, with big crowds attending, was attracting decent sponsorship with Texaco coming on board. The following year saw The Martins Group as co-sponsors whereby they were able to bring such luminaries as Barry Sheene, Patrick Tambay and James Hunt. The queue to get in stretched all the way back to Croft on Tees some years and it was a staple of the schedule until Croft Autodrome closed in 1981.

In recent years D&DMC have revived the Battle of Britain title and still combine all disciplines of two-, three- and four-wheel motorsport on the traditional August date at Croft.

And while Croft will forever be synonymous for the association with the Battle of Britain meetings, after those early ventures at Thornaby and Catterick, Rufforth near York also staged Battle of Britain events for cars only whereby their very final event was held on 4 September 1977.

Above: Barry Sheene paid a visit to Croft Autodrome for the 1980 Battle of Britain meeting with girlfriend Stephanie and stepson Roman as passengers. (Tony Todd)

Right: James Hunt was the special guest at the 1976 meeting in the same year he won the World Formula One title. (Tony Todd)

The Battle of Britain meetings were a fixture at many northern circuits over the years. (Cartersport)

French Formula One star Patrick Tambay attended in 1978 and was persuaded to take to the wheel of Andy Barton's Formula Libre car. (Tony Todd)

The start of a Formula Ford race in 1975, which always provided lots of excitement. (Terry Wright)

STARS OF THE FUTURE: FAMOUS NAMES STARTING OUT

For every marathon winner, it starts with a single step, so the old adage goes. Everyone has to start somewhere and who knows where those tentative first laps may lead.

The Guards Formula Three meeting at Croft in 1970 heralded the start of some impressive careers of the likes of Carlos Pace, James Hunt, Niki Lauda, Wilson Fittipaldi, and company, while four years previously, arguably a meeting of even greater prestige was held with the WD and HO Wills Trophy Meeting in 1966, which included the likes of Bruce McLaren, Denny Hulme, Chris Amon, John Surtees, Brian Redman, Peter Gethin, Innes Ireland, and David Hobbs.

The year 1971 saw the Formula Three rules change from the highly tuned 1-litre cars to the new 1,600 cc rules and the Rothmans International Trophy Race Meeting in mid-July saw Croft host round five of the series.

As usual it was a truly international affair and arriving in North Yorkshire with an 8-point lead was thirty-year-old Australian Dave Walker in the Ford-powered works Gold Leaf Lotus. Second was up-and-coming British driver Roger Williamson in his first season of single-seaters in Tom Wheatcroft's Holbay-engined March with little-known American Sandy Shepard (Brabham Holbay) third.

With the British GP at Silverstone and following Formula Three round at Cadwell Park the week after, the meeting saw a forty-one-car grid assemble for the two heats and thirty-lap final with prize money of £200 for the winner.

The opening ten-lap heat saw Walker ease to victory ahead of Swede Ulf Svensson's Brabham and the factory-entered Chevron of Barrie Maskell in third. Fourth went the way of a twenty-three-year-old by the name of James Hunt (March) with Shepard in fifth. Sixth place went to Swedish driver Conny Andersson with British ace David Purley in seventh and Dr Joe Ehrlich's unique prototype EMC 606 driven by South African Jody Scheckter. Ehrlich, an Austrian who fled from Vienna in the 1930s, also produced motorcycles which raced in the various World Championships over the years.

Heat two saw Williamson take the win ahead of British driver Andy Sutcliffe (Lotus 69 Holbay) with Brazilian Rikki Von Opel in third in a similar car as they headed into the final.

With Walker on pole position, thirty fast and furious laps followed, and at the flag Walker took the victory to extend his lead in the series. Hunt came home in second place ahead of Maskell and the Ensign of late replacement driver, Alan Rollinson, as Svensson and Shepard completed the top six.

Frank Gardner (5,700 cc Chevrolet Camaro) won the supporting thirty-five lap RAC British Touring Car Championship race at the same meeting with John Miles (Chevron B19) victorious in both Jock Leith Trophy Races for Sports Cars.

Of course, both Hunt and Scheckter would go on to be crowned Formula One World champions later in the decade whereas Roger Williamson would tragically lose his life at the Dutch GP just two years later in harrowing scenes beamed live on television as David Purley tried to upright the burning car on his own without success. Purley, heir to the LEC Refrigeration empire, was awarded the George Medal for his heroic efforts to save Williamson but died in an aerobatic plane crash in 1985 near his home on the south coast.

Over the years many drivers, and indeed riders, have cut their teeth on northern circuits including Kimi Räikkönen, Jensen Button and a certain Lewis Hamilton, who was making a name for himself back in 2003 when he did the double in a Formula Three meeting at Croft. I wonder what became of him...

Whereas the burgeoning car racing fraternity tended to stick to the more southern circuits out of preference, although a few did venture north on occasions, in the two- and three-wheeled worlds the racetracks of the north were the chosen battlefields for the emerging racers clad in leather.

Double 500 cc world champion Barry Sheene made more than one journey up to Croft in the late 1960s from his London home and of course became an institution just 50 miles to the east at Oliver's Mount. The switchback Scarborough track was in stark contrast to the wide-open spaces of the developing Grand Prix arenas and for all his criticism of places like the Isle of Man TT and Ulster Grand Prix, he was a big fan of Oliver's Mount and rarely missed a meeting.

Contrastingly, Sheene once said of the 14.1-mile Nürburgring circuit that he raced on during his World Championship career: 'You'd have to be William Tell to hit a straw bale around here', but he never had any qualms about Oliver's Mount where there is now a plaque commemorating his successes adjacent to the start/finish line.

One of Sheene's main protagonists was Yorkshireman Mick Grant, who was a regular visitor to Croft at the start of his career. Grant enjoyed lots of success on his way to a stellar career as a Kawasaki factory rider who will be ever associated with the 'green-meanies'.

Ken Redfern and Mac Hobson too, depicted elsewhere in this book, cut their teeth on the local ribbon of tarmac just south of the River Tees, with many race victories before their careers were cut tragically short. One time Redfern crashed on the opening lap of a race and by the time he'd straightened his battered bike and remounted, he was almost a lap down, yet he blitzed his way through the field to win.

Croft hosted a number of rounds of the British Solo Championship from the mid-1970s, which attracted many of the stars to North Yorkshire. The likes of Steve Parrish, who went on to become a teammate of Sheene's for a number of years in the factory Suzuki Grand Prix squad, was a regular, so too Ron Haslam, Roger Marshall, George Fogarty (World Superbike champion Carl's dad), Keith Huewen and Geoff Barry.

They'd be up against an awesome display of local talent from the region surrounding Croft such as local riders including Alan Stewart, John Webb, Stewart Hodgson, Mark Middleton, Andy McGladdery, Geoff Johnson, Neil Mason, John Wilson, Chris Hopes, John France, and Graham Petite to name a few.

The 1977 British Solo Championship at Croft will go down in local folklore as one of the best ever bike races around the 1.75-mile airfield circuit. It was a red-hot Whitsuntide May bank holiday weekend with two heats to decide the forty finalists such was the entry of ninety riders.

Rocket Ron, on the 750 cc Pharaoh Yamaha, took the first heat ahead of Roger Marshall's Mel Farrer 750 cc Yamaha with the Grosvenor Yamaha 750 of Steve Manship in third, while in heat two Geoff Barry (Sid Griffiths Racing Yamaha), Mick Spivey (Revoc Yamaha) and Bill Swales on the GT Garages Yamaha all made it through to give a taste of things to come.

The final itself was a classic, tinged with a little controversy, over ten laps with the lead constantly changing. Lap after lap, Haslam and Marshall swapped places at the front, upping the lap record on a couple of occasions as they fought for supremacy.

Arriving on the scene where Manship had crashed and was being attended to by medics, Marshall braked upon seeing the yellow flag, but an unsighted Haslam didn't, and he held on to take the chequered flag. Spivey finished third ahead of Fogarty's 500 cc Suzuki with the 350 cc Yamahas of Steve Wright and Kevin Stowe completing the top six.

There was another round later that year in September at Croft also, when the planned meeting at Brands Hatch was cancelled, and although Marshall was absent contesting an event overseas, main rival Alan Stewart couldn't secure the victory he needed meaning Marshall went on to win his second title in three years to add to the one he secured in 1975.

Sadly, although victory went to Yorkshireman Steve Wright at that meeting, it will be remembered for promising young talent Phil Bosco losing his life when he crashed at the Barcroft section of the track.

A cheeky young Barry Sheene was an occasional visitor up north at the start of his career. (Mortons Archive)

The start of the British Solo Championship race at Croft in 1976 with future stars Steve Manship, Geoff Barry, Steve Parrish, Roger Marshall, Mick Patrick, and Stan Woods. (Tony Todd)

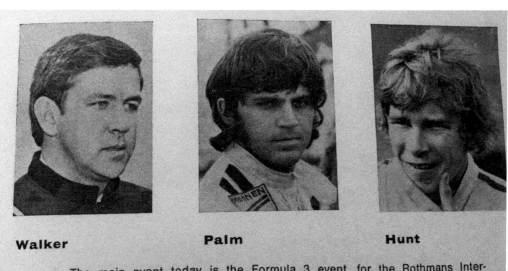

Walker   **Palm**   **Hunt**

The main event today is the Formula 3 event, for the Rothmans International Trophy. The BARC had orignally planned to run this in two parts, with results calculated on aggregate race times, but so great was the demand for entries that instead it was decided to run two heats of 10 laps each and a 30-lap final. A great many foreign drivers — easily outnumbering the British contingent — have boosted the entry list to a terrific 41 cars, many of the foreigners having decided to take in Croft on their way to the Woolmark British GP Meeting at Silverstone next weekend. Many of them are also staying on for two more BARC meetings, the Europe Cup FV, Cadwell, the day after the GP, and the Kodak Formula 5000, Thruxton, on August 1st.

James Hunt raced at Croft at the start of his career. This is a profile previewing him and other future Formula One stars at the 1971 Rothmans Trophy meeting. (Cartersport)

In the year he won his second 500 cc World Championship in 1977, Barry Sheene raced at Oliver's Mount, Scarborough. Also pictured is Dave Potter (6), Steve Manship (9), Pat Hennen (3), Bernie Murray (23) and Steve Parrish (1). (Nick Nicholls at Mortons Archive)

Lewis Hamilton won a pair of Formula Renault races at Croft in 2003 before going on to multiple World Formula One titles. (Tony Todd)

THE 1977 LOMBARD RAC RALLY: WALDEGARD WINS

One annual event always captured the nation's imagination every November because, quite simply, instead of you having to go to a sporting event, it came to you. And you couldn't help being caught up in it all because it sometimes passed your home/workplace, or in my case school, the cars passed you in a traffic jam or you stood at an unearthly hour on a roundabout or bridge just to see everyday cars with numbers on the side drive past.

Indelibly associated with sponsors Lombard for its formative years, the RAC Rally became an institution that led to many a teenage racer becoming besotted with cars, whether it be them trundling from stage to stage on a road section (where all traffic laws and speed limits had to be observed) or echoing off trees in light-emblazoned forests or stately homes up and down the country.

As well as the razzmatazz that these cosmopolitan warriors brought to the locality, there was a more important aspect to these events as well. The small matter of the World Rally Championship, and usually the deciding round, played out in the forest tracks of northern England.

Back in the mid-1970s, and perhaps for the next decade or so, the Lombard RAC Rally was a four- or five-day marathon, with 200 crews defying sleep as they threaded their way around the country covering 2,000 miles. Repairs effected in laybys on the roadside, Fords, Fiats, Vauxhalls, Toyotas, Triumphs, Saabs, Opels, Lancias, you name them, the manufacturers saw the importance of testing their latest models to the maximum. And if you win on Sunday, you sell on Monday and that's why the Manufacturers' world title was so important. In fact, 1977 was the first year there was a Drivers' championship that had been won in advance of the event by Italian Sandro Munari.

The 1977 event was another classic, with 182 of the world's best crews converging on the Wembley start on Sunday 20 November at 9 a.m. for the steady run north to York. Finn Pentti Airikkala (Vauxhall Chevette) was quickest on SS1 at Blenheim Palace with countryman Hannu Mikkola (Toyota Celica) fastest at Towcester Racecourse before Pentti hit back at Sutton Park in Birmingham. British hero Roger Clark set the fastest time on Tom's Hill near Tring with Airikkala fastest again at Donington Park.

Mikkola was quickest in Blidworth and Clipstone forests near Mansfield with Ari Vatanen's Ford Escort sharing fastest times at the second Clipstone test and RAF Finningley. Darkness and frost were descending when Stig Blomqvist stopped the clocks quickest at Bramham Park, but it was Mikkola who led at the York Racecourse halt. Estimates suggested upwards of a million spectators had witnessed the Sunday action before the real rally began on Monday morning.

A long trip over to the Welsh forests via the tests of another spin around Bramham Park and then Oulton Park and the Great Orme saw Mikkola hold the lead, but as soon as the rally hit the proper forests of north Wales, Bjorn Waldegard was making his presence felt in his Ford Escort RS1800. Little did anyone know it at the time, but the Swede wouldn't be headed as he swept to victory. But a lot of miles were to expire as his rivals battled against the miserable British winter weather and the clock, and by Tuesday evening thirty-seven stages were in the bag with Waldegard heading Mikkola by 43 seconds with Britain's Russell Brookes third in his Ford half a minute further back.

A welcome few hours in bed in York soon passed before weary crews headed out at dawn via stages in Kilburn, Boltby, Croft and Stang, where Waldegard was fastest on all to extend his lead, before heading over to the Lake District. Legendary places such as Grizedale, Greystoke and Whinlatter took their toll before crews headed further north through the day and night into Scotland.

As if places like Castle O'Er, Twiglees, Wellcleuch, White Naze, Glenhill, Glentress, Elibank and Yarr in the snow weren't enough in the middle of the night, they had to tackle four stages in 'Killer' Kielder and a monster 11 miler in Hamsterley before a breakfast halt at the now-defunct Dragonara Hotel in Middlesbrough.

Waldegard and co-driver Hans Thorszelius had extended their lead to nearly 2 minutes over Mikkola and Arne Hertz as the final sting in the tail was played out in the Yorkshire forests, thankfully in daylight. Airikkala and British champion-elect Brookes couldn't be separated in Ingleby with Simo Lampinen's Fiat 131 quickest in Cropton and Gayle Hill (Gale Rigg).

Roger Clark and Stuart Pegg gave the massive crowd in Dalby something to cheer with fastest time over the 15 miler before Waldegard shared fastest time in Staindale with new world champion Sandro Munari (Lancia Stratos). Andy Dawson (Ford) and Lampinen shared quickest time in the penultimate test in Langdale before Munari put a host of problems on the event to bed with outright fastest time in Wykeham as the crews headed back to York for the 4 p.m. finish.

Bjorn Waldegard in action during Sunday's spectator stages in his British Airways-backed Ford Escort. (Cartersport)

Waldegard took the honours as darkness descended, 2 and a half minutes ahead of Mikkola and Brookes third. The 1976 winner, Clark, salvaged fourth ahead of Dawson and Finn Kyösti Hämäläinen to make it five Escorts in the top six. But it wasn't enough to wrest the final Manufacturers' standings from Fiat, who nicked the title by 4 points.

Just sixty-seven intrepid crews made the finish, which would have been sixty-eight had Terry Kaby's Triumph Dolomite not blown a head gasket on the final stage, and having got stuck in traffic on the way back to York was OTL (outside total lateness) by just 4 minutes. How cruel the sport can be!

Right: Sandro Munari didn't enjoy the 1977 Lombard RAC Rally but had already won the inaugural World Driver's Championship in his Lancia Stratos. (Cartersport)

Below: A promotional flyer relating to various aspects of the 1977 event. (Cartersport)

Above: Winners Bjorn
Waldegard (right)
and co-driver Hans
Thorszelius celebrate
at the York finish.
(Cartersport)

Left: A service
pass from the 1977
Lombard RAC Rally.
(Cartersport)

LOCAL SPEEDWAY: DOING THE ROUNDS

Underneath the spiralling ribbon of roads where the A66 dissects the A19 at the southern end of the Tees flyover lies a piece of British sporting history.

The site of Cleveland Park Stadium on Stockton Road in Middlesbrough may now be home to the Goals complex of artificial soccer pitches owned by MacMillan College, but for much of the twentieth century it was an integral part of Teesside heritage hosting both greyhound and speedway racing.

It began life in 1928 when Jack French formed the National Greyhounds Middlesbrough Ltd on an 11-acre site of former allotments in the Ayresome Ward, just south of the River Tees, and from then onwards dogs and bikes attracted decent crowds over the years, despite one or two interruptions and relocations, before it finally closed its doors at the end of 1996.

The speedway team was renowned for showcasing local talent over the years under the guises of Middlesbrough Bears, The Teessiders and Teesside Tigers, and enjoyed plenty of success, the highlight being winning the National League Championship in 1981.

As well as traditional league competitions, the track hosted a number of high-profile individual meetings with large crowds very much in attendance on the traditional Thursday evenings. Many people had just got paid so cash through the track turnstiles followed by a pint in the Speedway Hotel in West Lane afterwards was a way of life for many.

One of those meetings was the end-of-season Battle of Britain Trophy in September 1963, which was a memorable time for the Bears fans. Just three weeks earlier, New Zealander Ivan Mauger, riding for Newcastle Diamonds and who would go on to win six world titles, set the four-lap course record.

Then the week after reigning world champion Peter Craven wowed the Teesside crowd again by setting a new three-lap course record in a match versus Norwich. Sadly, Craven lost his life in an accident while competing at Edinburgh just a week after his appearance at Cleveland Park.

The Bears had endured mixed fortunes in 1963 and ended the Provincial League season third bottom after a series of injuries to key riders had plagued their season. So, the chance to shine on home soil was a great incentive for the Bears, who were up against riders from Newcastle, Cradley Heath and Long Eaton.

Newcastle's Mike Watkin won the opening heat before Middlesbrough skipper Eric Boocock took heat two. Long Eaton's Australian sensation Bluey Scott was victorious in heat three, while Cradley Heath rider Ivor Brown took the flag in heat four. John Mills edged out Bears teammate Boocock in heat five before Brown defeated Watkin in heat six. Boro's Clive Hitch took heat seven with Heathen Ivor Davies winning heat eight. Alan Butterfield for the Bears claimed heat nine prior to the interval.

The meeting continued through the second half, including Middlesbrough riders Jack Swales, Maurice Tate, the emerging Dave Younghusband, Kevin Torpie and John Fitzpatrick all getting on the scorecard as the meeting progressed.

So, on to the final heat, which saw Boocock needing to defeat Brown in order to force a 'run-off' for the prestigious title and trophy, which had kindly been donated by the Middlesbrough branch of RAFA. Younghusband was there to try to assist his teammate while Coventry's Matt Mattox was a late replacement for Newcastle Diamonds star Brian Craven.

With the crowd on tenterhooks and cheering for the hometown skipper, Boocock did what he needed and edged out Brown to win and, with both riders on 14 points and Scott back on 13 points, it was down to a two-rider run-off to determine the title.

However, the drama wasn't over. As Boocock arrived at the tapes there was no sign of Heathen's captain Brown, whose machine was suspected of developing a mechanical fault, so the crown went to Yorkshire-born Boocock by means of a 'walkover'.

Following the 1964 season, Bears' promoter Reg Fearman opened up a speedway track at the Shay in Halifax and moved his Middlesbrough riders, including Boocock, there to form the Halifax Dukes. It meant league speedway was absent from Cleveland Park until 1968 where it remained until the last meeting in September 1996.

There was another interesting meeting at Cleveland Park on Thursday 1 August 1974 when the Tigers took on and hosted local rivals Berwick, Sunderland, and Workington in a Four Team Tournament. This constituted four matches in four days with the following legs at Sunderland on the Friday, Berwick on the Saturday, and Workington on the Sunday afternoon.

Having won the title the previous year, the match at Middlesbrough proved a close-run thing as victory for Jim Wells of Sunderland in heat one was followed by a win for Denny Mortar for Berwick in heat two. Tigers' Bruce Forrester took heat three with Workington's Mitch Graham winning heat four. The Cumbrians took heat five with Alan Cowland before Forrester took his second win in heat six. Graham responded in heat seven with Tigers' Pete Reading claiming heat eight.

At the halfway point, Sunderland and Workington shared the lead on 14 points each with Middlesbrough a point further back on thirteen and Berwick adrift in fourth on 7 points.

Middlesbrough's Dave Durham bolstered local hopes with a win in heat nine, but Graham took his third win of the night in heat ten. Heat eleven saw Russ Hodgson crash out for the Tigers as Workington's Mal Mackay took the win, but Forrester reduced the deficit with his third victory of an enthralling meeting in heat twelve. But the home team's hopes were effectively scuppered when Hodgson crashed out of heat thirteen as Steve Watson took maximum points for Workington.

Graham rounded off a perfect night with his fourth win in heat fourteen and before teammate Cowland romped to victory in the penultimate heat to make it an unbeatable 6-point gap in the favour of Workington. Durham won the last heat to give the Tigers second place ahead of Sunderland, who had local Teesside aces Brian Havelock and Tim Swales in their ranks, with Berwick a disappointing fourth.

Middlesbrough won ahead of the home team at Sunderland the following night before doing likewise at Berwick on the Saturday. Workington trounced the Tigers by a massive 23 points at home in the final leg to claim the trophy overall with the final tallies being Workington 122, Middlesbrough 110, Sunderland 90, and Berwick 62.

Above: The Middlesbrough Bears team from 1963. (Cartersport)

Right: Action from a packed Cleveland Park when the Boro Bears took on Wolverhampton Wolves in a 1964 meeting. (Cartersport)

REG AND HIS BEARS BID YOU AU REVOIR UNTIL 1964

ERIC BOOTHROYD

JOHN FITZPATRICK

ERIC BOOCOCK

CLIVE HITCH

DAVE YOUNGHUSBAND

KEVIN TORPIE

BRIAN McKEOWN

FRED GREENWELL

Rider profiles from the final programme of 1963. (Cartersport)

Programme cover from the 1974 Four Team Tournament. (Cartersport)

The 1963 Battle of Britain Trophy programme cover. (Cartersport)

STOCK CARS MOVE INTO THE MODERN ERA: THE AMERICAN DREAM

In the very basic of analogies, stock car racing is the four-wheeled version of speedway in as much as they compete on oval tracks, and usually on shale. That's where the comparisons end, however, as the races in stock cars are much longer, involve a lot more competitors and it is encouraged to crash into each other – hence the armour and large bumpers on the cars to 'assist' with the passing moves.

In the British Stock Car Association (abbreviated to BriSCA), drivers are graded by their previous performances and allocated a roof colour accordingly. The highest group is that of 'Superstar' (red), which means for virtually every race; the 'red roofs' have to start the oval races at the back of the field and work their way through. It inevitably leads to contact and spinning someone out, known in the trade as 'putting the bumper in', but is commonplace and part and parcel of the game.

Despite its popularity and longevity, stock car racing remains the crudest of motorsport disciplines when it comes to commercialism. Cold and windy stadiums, many decrepit and in some cases condemned, limited media coverage and even less on television although a hard core and loyal following of fans would disagree with its seeming lack of appeal.

The sport has occasionally flirted with mainstream publicity and there have been a couple of high-profile attempts to bring it kicking and screaming into the modern era. One memorable time was back in 1985 when young local driver Paul Broatch from Bedale was establishing himself, larger-than-life Hartlepool Raceway promoter Warren Taylor tied up a sensational and unique deal with United States Tobacco International, one of whose brands was the smokeless tobacco sachets, Skoal Bandits, which were so popular in the USA.

It coincided with the product (now banned) being aggressively marketed in the UK, and with an impressive budget to spend Taylor set up an F2 team that included Broatch. As part of the deal, Taylor included the 'Skoal Bandit Shoot Out' at Hartlepool Raceway during the 1985 season, which culminated in a lucrative 'Dash For Cash', which was won by multiple world champion Stu Smith.

Arriving at a windswept North East at the track that was located just south of and backed onto Hartlepool United's Victoria Park, complete with the chill of the North Sea,

Left: Paul Broatch raced in Skoal Bandit livery in 1985. (Neil Pinkney)

Below: At a time when sponsorship was rare, the American ideal was brought over to the UK, but it was short-lived. (Neil Pinkney)

were NASCAR driver Harry Gant, complete with 10-gallon cowboy hat, and Grand Prix motorcycle racer Rob McElnea with his immaculate Suzuki RG500.

There was also IndyCar star Tom Sneva, who won the Indianapolis 500 two years previous, with the newly developed Indy Eagle 85GC for Dan Gurney's Curb-All American Racers team. His satin white jacket with the Skoal Masked Bandit logo embroidered on the chest and a large version of the Bandit on the back wasn't really in keeping with a hard-working northern English industrial hub where local authority donkey jackets were more the order of the day.

A show model of Gant's Skoal Bandit-liveried No. 33 Mach 1 Racing Chevrolet was on display at the track during the season while the merchandise and concession stands were as good in Hartlepool as they were at Daytona. And with fans buying into the concept, there was money to be made off track as well as on it.

However, rubbing shoulders with American NASCAR and IndyCar stars and adrenaline-fuelled GP racers at events and promotions during the season, with all the razzmatazz of the American dream thrown in, was a little too far removed from the humble origins of the sport that began in the UK in 1954 and it fizzled out.

That's not to say the sport hasn't prospered and over the years, as various events have increased in prestige, decent prize money has been up for grabs.

A rather unusual handwritten programme cover from the Autumn Trophy meeting in November 1985 at Hartlepool Stadium. (Cartersport)

The grid lines up for a race at the now defunct Aycliffe Stadium in 1975. (Tony Todd)

Minimal crowd protection, crudely constructed cars but the spectacle has always been the same. Aycliffe 1975. (Tony Todd)

SCRAMBLING MECCAS: OFF-ROADERS

Back in the day, off-road racetracks in the region were almost as common as days in the week. The bountiful locations were testament to the local undulating topography, which meant on most weekends you could find some event or other on without venturing too far.

That 'day' would have been anytime between the 1950s, when good old British scrambling morphed into the future by adopting the French word 'moto-cross', through to the 1980s as the sport arguably hit its peak of popularity.

Places like Carlton Bank in the Cleveland foothills, Woodhouse Farm at Great Ayton, Hutton Conyers near Ripon and Hunters Hill Farm at Nether Silton, all regularly hosted events, not to mention the forgotten tracks at Hailstone Moor and Target Wood in the Bullamoor region of Northallerton.

Not only that, but the star names of the times, many of them local, and quite often the television cameras rocked up too, to expose North Yorkshire and the surrounding areas in all its natural glory.

They've mostly disappeared now. A combination of commercial or domestic developments proved more lucrative than permit fees in some cases, changes of landownership in others. But probably the biggest reason was the increased burden for organisers regarding stifling HSE and insurance legislation as well as the increasing pressure by the environmental lobby.

While there are a few notable exceptions that remain, mainly out towards the East Coast at Pickering, Whitby, and Scarborough, as well as Thirsk & District Motor Club continuing to use arch-motorsport enthusiast Derek Cornforth's land at the top of Sutton Bank, other than an odd outline on Google Earth, only memories remain.

Two other major venues in the area, which like Carlton Bank hosted British championship action in the region, have also been condemned to the annals of history, Boltby and Howe Hills.

Anyone who has traversed the terrifying ascent of Sneck Yate Bank at the foot of the Yorkshire Moors will vouch for the gradient between the low-lying and quaint village of Boltby near Thirsk and the top of the Hambleton Hills. Thus, the landscape to the west, on the fringes of the famous forest, made an ideal motocross course, in fact a world-class one that had hosted events since 1945.

One such occasion was the penultimate round of the 1989 British Championship which saw Northallerton and District Motor Club team up with their counterparts from Thirsk to organise the event on Mr Stephen Gilchrist's estate. The best riders in the UK attracted a massive crowd to watch them do battle over eight races as reigning champion Kurt Nicoll and main rival Dave Thorpe went head-to-head for the crown.

However, it was KTM rider Brian Wheeler who took the overall victory on the day with local riders Jared Smith from Guisborough and Bishop Auckland's Carl Shaw also in action as well as a number of other locals in the qualifying championship.

Just over a decade earlier, in the summer of 1978, another big motocross meeting was staged in the region, this time at the Howe Hills circuit near Sedgefield. Again, a host of top names, many to later become world champions, descended on the tortuous County Durham track, noted for its difficult and unforgiving terrain.

The motor clubs of Northallerton and Middlesbrough put on a great event with Neil Hudson taking the first 'moto' ahead of Graham Noyce, with Noyce getting his revenge in the second outing over 40 minutes plus two laps later in the day. Both riders would go on to win world titles within the next couple of years while local honour was upheld that day by Barnard Castle-based Scot, Jimmy Aird.

Nowadays, it's mainly walkers and mountain bikers who get to use the Boltby forest complex, and the adjacent team room at High Paradise Farm is popular with the outdoor clientele, while a stable yard and racing thoroughbreds of one horsepower each fill the fields of Howe Hills. A contrast in both cases compared to where those two-wheeled gladiators once battled it out for supremacy.

Above: Graham Noyce was the man to beat in the 1970s, including taking a victory at Howe Hills in County Durham in 1978. (Mortons Archive)

Left: A mud-splattered Jimmy Aird from Barnard Castle in action in 1968. (Mortons Archive)

Neil Hudson was another rider to sample victory at the 1978 British Championship meeting at Howe Hills. (Mortons Archive)

The start of a motocross race at Hunters Hill Farm, Nether Silton in 1974. (Tony Todd)

BRITISH MOTOCROSS CHAMPIONSHIPS

MOTOR cycle WEEKLY

incorporating
THE CLEVELAND GRAND NATIONAL

HOWE HILLS
Moto~Cross Circuit
SUNDAY, 9th. JULY
1978

Promoted by
NORTHALLERTON & DISTRICT MOTOR CLUB
and MIDDLESBROUGH & DISTRICT MOTOR CLUB 20p

The programme cover from Howe Hills in 1978. The venue is now a horse racing stable. (Cartersport)

THE LOCAL HERO: ALEX CLACHER AND THE BBC SHOW

When you live just a couple of miles away from a racetrack and have a passion for sport on two and four wheels, it's inevitable that at some point you'll end up competing.

Alex Clacher was one such person who just happened to be very good on both bikes and in cars. He started off riding trials bikes, even appearing on the cover of the Scott Trial programme for 1961. With good friend Bill Hocking's help, he was able to move into motocross or 'scrambling' as it was then known.

He began car racing with the first of his legendary Imps, which was written off in a pile-up on the start line at Oulton Park before a second car, an ex-Reg Hargraves Imp, arrived in 1971. In the four years he owned it, he brought his lap times round his local Croft Autodrome circuit down by about 8 seconds.

Later in that period he travelled to more distant circuits, setting half a dozen lap records, from Brands Hatch in Kent to Ingliston in Scotland, often on his first visit. He was known as a smooth, very fast driver and quick to learn a new circuit. He took as much interest in developing the car as in driving it and most of the work was done in his garage at home.

Perhaps his legacy is best remembered for his epic 1,000 cc saloon car battles around Croft in particular with two counterparts who were equally talented and just as determined. Cast your minds back to the early 1970s where on many occasions, at a windswept and desolate North East racetrack, there was many a live show better than anything on telly, with an unsuspecting cast of drivers and machinery.

Take an up-and-coming Geordie, throw in a Cumbrian mechanic and a Croft-on-Tees-based Scot with a funny-sounding name. Add in a couple of small engined Minis and a Hillman Imp and you had a recipe for some of the finest ever saloon car racing ever witnessed at Croft, so much so they named it 'The BBC Show'.

The first 'B' in the acronym is Barton. In the early programmes listed as Andrew, Andy became one of the most successful drivers of all time at Croft. The garage proprietor from Newburn on Tyneside had campaigned a Morris 1,000 and a Mini Marcos during the mid-1960s before building one of his many powerful Mini Coopers. The 850 cc Holbay-engined version proved to be very competitive and with his distinctive hand-painted numbers and three-wheeling antics through the corners, he became a firm crowd favourite before moving onto single seaters in his later career.

Sedric Bell, who also owned a garage, lived in Carlisle and was the quiet man of racing despite being sponsored by the Cosmopolitan Club in Harraby. Nicknamed 'The Cosmo', the nightspot hosted such luminaries as The Who, Pink Floyd and The Moody Blues in the 1960s. Such was the impression he made on his many trips across the A66, that Darlington and District Motor Club inaugurated a trophy in his memory in 2009, after his untimely death from Parkinson's disease.

Then of course there was Clacker. Or was it Clasher? No one seemed to know but the tall, bespectacled plumber was often entered (as his Darlington business which has operated since 1961 attests) as A. J. Clacher, but to his friends he was simply Alex.

The cars they raced were engineering masterpieces with many modifications way ahead of their time. Back then, the predominant class in British motor racing was Formula Three, which was limited to 1,000 cc maximum engines so most of the development work was centred around that capacity. Various versions included Barton's 1972 Mini Cosworth SCA 997 cc and Bell's Mini-Holbay Ford F3 997 cc, which were reputed to churn out over 140 bhp.

On one occasion, the usual 'BBC' battle was in full flight at Croft when Clacher suffered a rare mechanical failure. That left Bell and Barton to scrap it out for the lead and as they exited the chicane, they were side by side. With the dividing barrier between the pits and start line rapidly approaching and neither driver prepared to yield, Bell ended up going flat out down the pitlane, changing up gears as he went

Pictured at Ingliston, a rare colour image of Alex Clacher in one of his legendary Imps. (Tony Todd)

as Barton followed the track. Sedric was black-flagged and incurred the wrath of the officials afterwards.

Another battle occurred at the first race meeting of the 1973 season at Croft when all three scrapped it out in a ten-lap MCD Special Saloon Championship race. Barton got the verdict ahead of Clacher with Bell in third, but there was never much between them. All three travelled to other tracks, including Rufforth near York and Ingliston near Edinburgh having plenty of success at those places too, but it's those battles at Croft that remain indelibly etched in the memory.

While the entertainment factor was always paramount between those three, let's not forget the other saloon car stalwarts who plied their trade locally such as the Mini of Ken Walker; the two Tonys, Dickinson and Sugden, in their radical Skoda 130s, John Blankley's Rockside A40, Keith Bowmaker's V8 Escort and of course, Chris Meek and Doug Niven's various thundering creations. Leeds businessman Meek drove just about anything he could get his hands on while Scotsman Niven, the late Jim Clark's cousin, rocked up in the likes of Ford Boss Mustangs, Escorts and even a 5-litre V8 Chevrolet-engined VW Beetle.

Some of the cars live on, as do some of the drivers and can be seen occasionally at the various classic or retro meetings these days. But they'll never recreate those indelible memories of three working class lads in their home-built specials who entertained those lucky enough to witness it.

Tall, bespectacled, and quietly spoken, once in the cockpit of the car, 'A. J.' became a fierce competitor, seen here collecting the winner's garland at Croft. (Tony Todd)

The defining image of 1970s 1-litre Special Saloon racing: Barton, Bell and Clacher in that order at the Croft Chicane, the 'BBC Show' in typical close action. (Tony Todd)

Camaraderie at its finest: Sedric Bell, having retired from the race, gives the thumbs up to Clacher as he crosses the finish line at Croft. (Tony Todd)

No circuit garages to work in back then, Clacher (left) and some friends change the engine on the Imp in the Croft paddock. Note the Ford Cortina GXL in the background. (Tony Todd)

LOCAL LADY RACERS: GIRL POWER

Motorsport is one of the few sports that has been traditionally male-oriented over the years. At least on the face of it, rightly or wrongly, that's the long-held perception.

Its testosterone-fuelled image was of macho men defying death one minute before being garlanded in silverware the next and then leaving in a Roller with the latest Miss World (remember that?) and heading for the penthouse of a luxury hotel to 'relax'.

The stuff of movies and dreams, and a Boy's Own aspiration for spotty young lads to drape posters of the handlebar-moustachioed Graham Hill on their bedroom walls, the Playboy extraordinaire that was James Hunt, the solicitous Ayrton Senna, the methodical genius of Michael Schumacher via Mansell, Button and Hamilton. And the Hollywood stars such as Steve McQueen and James Garner who portrayed these stereotypical and heroic characters on the big screen.

But all is not what it seems because female participation is very much a part of life in the fast lane these days, and if you delve into the history books, then the ladies have always had a prominent role in various aspects of the sport.

Stirling Moss's sister Pat and Irish lady Rosemary Smith were pioneers in rallying and very talented drivers in the 1950s. South African Desire Wilson became the first (and so far, only) lady to win in Formula One when she took victory in a non-championship race at Brands Hatch in 1980. That decade also spawned French superstar Michele Mouton, who was at one point the best rally driver in the world in her fire-spitting Audi Quattro.

American Danica Patrick won an Indy Car race and set pole in NASCAR at Daytona while TV presenter Vicki Butler Henderson was every bit as good as her male counterparts on the track. On bikes, Spaniard Ana Carrasco won the World Supersport 300 Championship a couple of years ago, becoming the first female in history to achieve it; Jenny Tinmouth has lapped the TT course at an average speed of 120 mph; and Emma Bristow is a regular challenger on the world trials scene, to name but a few.

When it comes to the ladies, literally half the current Autograss paddock is comprised of a combination of junior girls, their mums and in some cases grandmothers. Trials feature an increasing number of both junior and senior females at all levels, not to mention the mass participation of girls in minibike racing or cadet karting. Rallying and rallycross, as well as circuit racing, enjoys the presence of women increasingly in their droves. And what's more this isn't tennis, soccer, golf, athletics, or cricket, etc., generally speaking there are few gender divisions or separate competitions defined by sex and so women usually race against men on equal terms and in equal machinery.

With regards to circuit racing, there have been plenty of ladies competing at local tracks including Croft, Catterick and Rufforth. Names such as Jill Hutchinson (Terrier), Jenny Birrell-Nadine (Wylie's Escort) and Gillian Fortescue-Thomas (Escort) plied their trade back in the 1960s and 1970s.

And then there was Valli. Real name Val Stack, she was a protégé of one of Croft's most successful drivers, Chris Meek, whereby the Leeds businessman helped procure sponsorship and ran her in the same teams as him for a couple of years in the mid-1970s. Meek realised the unique promotional and commercial value of having his girlfriend (at the time) race cars such as a Lotus Europa, a Triumph TR7 and an MG Midget and introduced such sponsors as Radio Luxembourg, Princess Ita and BIBA Cosmetics who bought into the concept. She had some pretty good results during her short career before marrying pop star Emile Ford (without his Checkmates, luckily).

Scots lass Kim Devine (Hillman Imp), local lady Helen Elstrop (Triumph Spitfire) and Jean Birkett (Rover Tomcat) were more recent combatants on track, while another local driver, Amanda Whitaker, really did take the sport by storm a couple of decades ago.

Originally from Newton Aycliffe, Whitaker became one of Britain's most successful female racing drivers, taking over fifty race wins and setting multiple lap records. During her tenure in the sport, she won numerous national single-seater titles, including the 2006 European Formula Atlantic Championship crown. Amanda was top points scorer overall in the European Formula Two Championship that year and became the first female in history to win a National Formula Ford Championship race.

Valli, MG Midget

Right: A fine, sunny day, 1970s fashion and the MG Midget she raced so successfully, 'Valli' poses in the Croft paddock. (Yvonne Wright)

Above: And seen here in action negotiating Oxo Bend at Croft. That part of the track is now behind the main spectator banking at Clervaux. (Yvonne Wright)

She then suffered a massive crash at Mallory Park, but it didn't faze her and soon she was back behind the wheel, just missing out by 3 points in the 2009 HSCC Formula Ford Championship. After she retired, Amanda became a performance driving instructor throughout the UK, Europe and USA working for most major manufacturers and racing schools as well as doing TV adverts.

Female trials riders have long been a tradition and these days there are as many lasses as lads competing, but going back a century it wasn't quite the norm. The first woman to start a Scott Trial was E. Knowles in 1921 and in 1926 Marjorie Cottle was the first female official finisher. It was her second attempt and she finished on a further three occasions, the last in 1931. From 1925 E. Foley entered six times but never finished, and before the Second World War a further eight women competed but none officially completed the course.

From 1950 to 2001 there were a further seven female riders, three making two attempts, and one entering three times, including Londoner Renee Bennett who was a regular competitor both in the Scottish Six Days Trial (SSDT) and the Scott Trial. Daughter of a motorcycle dealer who ended up running her own bike shop for many years with her husband who was a bodybuilding champion, Renee became a well-known figure for many decades on the national trials scene and in between events she was a part-time model advertising, among other things, Ovaltine in television adverts. How times have changed!

Jill Hutchinson poses for the camera at the wheel of her Terrier Mk 2 in the Ouston paddock. (Terry Wright)

And in action showing the effort needed to haul the car through the Ouston corners. The car was designed by Lotus engineer Len Terry and was one of very few built in 1960. (Terry Wright)

Chloe Richardson from Skeeby is just one of many ladies to have tackled the world-famous Scott Trial. Seen here at Orgate Falls. (Neil Sturgeon)

COASTAL GLADIATORS: SPEED ON THE SANDS

In the annals of history, the northern seaside towns of Saltburn and Redcar don't really stand out as major bastions of motorsport heritage, but going back a century they were very much to the fore.

Famous residents such as aspiring young TT ace Davey Todd, veteran racer Dave Woolams and former 500 cc Grand Prix crew chief Geoff Crust, who worked with the likes of world champions Wayne Rainey and Kevin Schwantz and whose father Ernie was the oracle of local racing aside. The beaches of the Cleveland Riviera are not where you'd expect to find such sporting excellence. But those very sands where these days dog walkers mingle with locals and tourists alike, along with the odd surfer, were once the scene of some popular and historic action on both two wheels and four.

The abundance of hard, smooth, and flat sands at Saltburn, or more accurately Agar's Gap to the north, which were several hundred feet wide at low tide, saw the adventurous pioneers descend with their fledgling jalopies starting with L. R. Anderson in July 1904, but it wasn't until two years later that things started to get more official and serious.

Having moved from Filey the previous year, 14 July 1906 saw an estimated 60,000 spectators witness Warrick Wright traverse the 2-mile course at a speed of 96.5 mph, but it was the following year that saw brewery heir Algernon 'Algy' Lee Guinness in his 200 hp French-built V8 Darracq take on the Dietrich of Maharajah Tikara. Guinness upped the speed on the course between Marske and Saltburn to over 111 mph despite atrocious weather before bettering it the year after to 121.6 mph, setting a new World Land Speed Record in the process.

In 1922, Malcolm Campbell went on to traverse the measured mile at an average of 138.08 mph, although timing anomalies deemed it not to be a record. But with increased speeds and the onset of the Second World War, plus a storm in 1938 that removed lots of sand and reduced the width that was available to the organisers, Saltburn was considered no longer suitable, so the action was moved up the coast to Redcar for racing to commence in 1946 after hostilities ceased.

Although there had been some record of racing at Redcar going back to the 1920s, the new course was based at Coatham and used the wide sweeping crescent of sand towards South Gare where tens of thousands of post-war fans would flock to watch both speed trials as well as sand racing. Mixtures of cars and motorcycles took part in the various competitions of differing lengths and disciplines, organised by Middlesbrough and District Motor Club.

One such meeting took place on Saturday 14 July 1951 and comprised fifteen events from a 3.15 p.m. start to the last race starting at 8 p.m. Over a hundred competitors converged with P. 'Harry' Shaw from York winning the 1-mile 250 cc solo motorcycle race on his Velocette to open proceedings, taking the £3 prize money also. J. Richmond from Darlington won the opening car event in a 1,496 cc HRG while another York Velocette rider, J. Benson won the 350 cc race.

Richmond's F. Harrison won the single-mile 1,500 cc car event in his 1,172 cc Ford Special with the 1-mile 600 cc bike event going to Manchester rider Reg Dearden on his 499 cc Norton. BSA works rider Fred Rist from nearby Stokesley won the 1-mile 1,000 cc event followed by another local rider, H. R. Walton from Middlesbrough, winning the 4-mile 200 cc solo race on his James.

An attempt at the 'Flying Kilometre Record for Motor Cycles' saw Darlington rider A. Roddam achieve a speed of 107.55 mph on his 998 cc Vincent HRD, but that didn't trouble the 136.40 mph set by George Brown the year previous.

Onto the 20-mile long 350 cc solo race for the East Yorkshire Championship which saw Fred Rist take the win for BSA ahead of Middlesbrough's J. F. Bean on a similar bike. However, in the corresponding event up to 600 cc machines, Rist had to give

Competitors unknown from a race meeting in 1922 as they turn left in front of some of Saltburn's landmarks. (Mortons Archive)

second best to the 499 cc Norton of Birmingham rider R.B. Young, each race winner netting a tenner.

Into the evening and the 10-mile 1,000 cc solo handicap race saw local rider D. Connett take victory on his 197 cc James before Harry Shaw won his second event of the day in the 250 cc 20 miler for the East Yorkshire Championship. The similar event for 1,000 cc machines, run concurrently, saw Fred Rist net his third win of the day with another £10 in prize money to boot.

The 20-mile 4,500 cc handicap race for cars saw Richmond's T. Sunter claim the win in his 3,442 cc Jaguar XK120 before claiming a superb double victory in the 10-mile Sports Car Race to close proceedings, bumping his winnings up to £16 as a result.

Racing ceased in 1955, but it was resurrected by local enthusiast Ernie Crust in 1962 and bike racing on the beach continued at Redcar for a number of years until a combination of financial, logistical, and operational factors saw the end of the action for good in the 1980s.

The cost of the programme for the July 1951 event was 1s with advertisers such as Uptons, Wm. Armstrong and Pallister, Yare & Cobb (all motorcycle dealers of Linthorpe Road, Middlesbrough), Wake's Pork Stores (Newport Road, Middlesbrough), Rea's Creamy Ices and Flemings of Redcar for Jaguar.

Another action shot from 1922 with the riders lined up to start with the Saltburn Scar rocky outcrop clearly defined. (Mortons Archive)

Right: The temporary scoreboard erected on Saltburn sands complete with hand-painted results for a 1922 meeting. (Mortons Archive)

Below: Competitors race around the course from Saltburn towards Marske with officials, dignitaries, and VIPs on the inside of the track, complete with cars from the early 1920s. (Mortons Archive)

Sand racing was popular at Coatham near Redcar in the 1950s, 1960s and 1970s before it gradually faded into obscurity. Here is a competitor in 1974 with the South Tees breakers in the background. (Tony Todd)

THE LOST TRACKS: GONE BUT NOT FORGOTTEN

Since the invention of the internal combustion engine, mankind's desire to pit himself and machinery against his counterparts has evolved into British motorsport boasting a rich and successful history that continues to this day.

The North East and Yorkshire has played a pivotal part in that development, with world champions from the region including Easingwold's Steve Webster who was World Sidecar champion ten times. Middleham's Andy Hetherington, along with driver Darren Dixon, were World Sidecar champions in 1995/1996 while Yarm's Gary Havelock sensationally won the World Speedway Championship in 1992.

Trials legend Dougie Lampkin is a twelve-times world champion while his dad Martin and Malcom Rathmell were other Yorkshiremen to literally rule the trials world. There are others who have attained richly deserved accolades thanks to plying their skills, bravery, and a little derring-do, including at local venues in the region.

Sadly, many of these bastions of power are no longer due to the march of progress over the generations, but for many the memories live on, while for those a little younger some of these places where motorsport took place may come as a surprise.

Post-war airfields were popular when it came to circuit racing and as well as Croft in its various guises over the years, racing took place at RAF Thornaby and RAF Catterick. Darlington and District Motor Club were instrumental in the organisation and between them and Middlesbrough and District Motor Club, hosted just four events at Thornaby, which comprised just 34 acres, between 1959 and 1960. Ormesby Hall in Middlesbrough once hosted racing in 1936 and so too did Albemarle Barracks (AKA Ouston) near Newcastle sporadically from the 1960s to the 1980s, but more about that later.

Catterick meanwhile, now part of Marne Barracks, was a venue from 1958 to 1963 until, it is alleged, a car spun off and ended up on the southbound carriageway of the A1 to end proceedings. Darlington driver Jimmy Blumer, who went on to race in Formula One, was a leading light at both Thornaby and Catterick during that time. Topcliffe, along with Full Sutton, Linton-on-Ouse and Rufforth, all near York, are now defunct racetracks.

That opening meeting at Catterick in 1958 saw 7,000 fans in attendance courtesy of the Air Ministry's Station Commander, Group Captain A. B. Riall who facilitated many of the military's resources to help run the meeting. Famous sports car driver Tony Lanfranchi started his racing career here while other well-known drivers from the Darlington area included Iestyn 'Doc' Williams and Campbell Dawson. Motorcycles also raced on the 1.6-mile triangular track including future world champion Dave Simmonds.

There was another venue at Catterick Camp which saw motorcycle racing in 1962 and 1963 with crowds of up to 10,000, and which was also part of the hill climb venue on the military roads of the Garrison near to Waithwith Bank. Darlington and District Motor Club hosted the first one in 1954 while the Christmas Stages Rally, organised since the 1970s by Northallerton Automobile Club, used those roads up until the turn of the millennium too. Middlesbrough and District Motor Club still occasionally use it as they do with organising the popular Saltburn Gathering, which incorporates runs up the famous bank from Cat Nab car park to the town centre at the top of the steep switchback hill.

Talking of hill climbs, many local village sports days used to incorporate a motorised aspect including the recently resurrected event at Bainbridge, which has attracted a massive crowd in recent years. Kilburn, as part of the 'Feast' along with Coxwold near Thirsk and Brompton near Northallerton were other places to host hill climbs and grass tracks.

Public roads were closed to allow competitors to tackle the hills at Sutton Bank, Swainby, Wass, Blue Bank near Whitby, Birk Brow, Rosedale Abbey (Chimney), Punchard Hill in Arkengarthdale and even Kirby Sigston while private roads at Scarth Nick near Osmotherley and Castle Howard were also used.

Indeed, motorcycle grass tracks were in abundance at places like Broomfield Showground in Northallerton with long-lost places such as Patrick Brompton, Faceby Lane Ends and Portrack Lane in Stockton seeing regular action. Sand racing at Coatham, Saltburn and Filey was popular with those world record attempts often being made on the local coastlines too. The Dales villages of Ovington and Newsham used to host archaic post-harvest stubble field banger racing every autumn, with the 'Demolition Derby' often ending in the dark.

Abandoned motocross courses proliferate and as far as rallying is concerned, the number of forests where competition is permitted nowadays are few and far between. I doubt you will ever see (Special Stage) rally cars in forests such as The Stang, Wykeham, Guisborough, Silton, Ingleby or Kilburn again.

The hill climb at Waithwith Bank on the Catterick military ranges proved popular with competitors and spectators alike. (Terry Wright)

Autograss tracks at Tunstall and Kiplin are no more, Stock Car ovals at Aycliffe, Barford and Hartlepool are gone too. Even local Speedway was lost at the historic Cleveland Park track in Middlesbrough back in the 1990s. There are dozens of others too numerous to mention of course, but as time marches on relentlessly, in its wake it leaves the glorious past which formed the foundations for an area still smitten by the motorsport bug.

Above: Competitors tackle an off-road hill climb at Gandale which formed part of the Catterick Garrison complex. (Terry Wright)

Right: A programme cover from a race meeting at Catterick Airfield in 1958. This is still adjacent to the A1 and now called Marne Barracks. (Terry Wright)

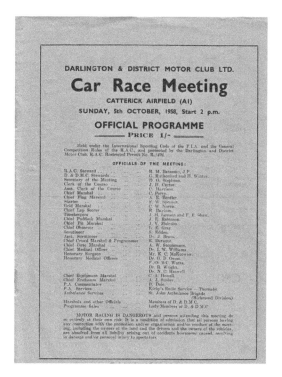

Darlington's only Formula One Grand Prix driver Jimmy Blumer in action at Catterick airfield in the 1950s. (Terry Wright)

Latterly, Catterick has hosted the popular Christmas Stages Rally around the various military roads of Europe's biggest army base. A multiple winner is Kevin Procter. (Tony Todd)

ALBEMARLE AND OUSTON: ENGLAND'S MOST NORTHERN TRACK

Racetracks in the north of England have always been few and far between, but one accolade that can be attributed to Ouston is that it was the last one before you reached the Scottish border.

Situated just 10 miles west of Newcastle Upon Tyne near the village of Stamfordham, the site was originally RAF Ouston before becoming Albemarle Barracks and was owned by the Ministry of Defence.

In late 1938, the Air Ministry evaluated the possibility of building an airfield adjacent to the hamlet bearing the same name just north of the Stanegate Roman Road to Carlisle. Construction work was slow to begin with because the area was quite remote from communication lines and there was some opposition from the local farming community, despite the land being quite low quality. A J-type hangar dominated the airfield, with the control tower situated in front of it.

The station opened on 10 March 1941 as a Fighter Sector HQ under No. 13 Group RAF (13 Gp) whereby the station's badge was a lion rampant in front of a Roman helmet. This was influenced by the nearby Hadrian's Wall and the lion is taken from the Percy family arms, who were local landowners.

Further squadrons during the Second World War included No. 317 Polish Fighter Squadron, No. 122 Squadron RAF (122 Sqn), No. 232 Squadron RAF arrived with Hurricanes and then No. 122 Sqn transferred to RAF Catterick in August 1941 and No. 131 Squadron RAF (131 Sqn) with a large proportion of Belgian pilots.

Various aircraft, from fighters to reconnaissance, occupied RAF Ouston flying coastal patrols and scrambles in defence of the North East as well as covering Air-Sea rescues. Combined with the nearby Otterburn military ranges, the base was used for training as much as actual conflict and was an important hub for the training of radar operators.

After the cessation of hostilities, RAF Ouston played a vital role as a training school and operating in a reserve role while the main hangar was used to service RAF equipment right up to 1961 when the site was disbanded. However, during the Cold War, as part of the nuclear deterrent, Ouston had its main runway extended to 1,800 metres and Operational Readiness Platforms added at each end of the extended runway.

It is reported that racing first took place at Ouston as early as 1961, but it is certain that the Newcastle and District Motor Club organised race meetings there in the summers of 1962, 1963 and 1964, the latter being a joint car and motorcycle event.

Scotsman Jackie Stewart was a competitor at the 1963 meeting driving a Jaguar E-Type where he won the race, and this is believed to have been his first victory. Jim Clark attended the meeting in 1964 and was driven round the circuit in an open-topped Jaguar E-Type and then presented the prizes so the story goes.

Sadly, the writing was on the wall for Ouston by then in 1964 as just down the road, Croft Autodrome had reopened, meaning the local car clubs and competitors concentrated their exploits there and four-wheeled racing was curtailed. However, bike racing continued for a couple of years more up in Northumberland where one race meeting, organised by the Newcastle Club and held in June 1965, reported that there were 20,000 spectators present.

The army took over the land and Albemarle Barracks were established on the site in 1970. The barracks were home to the Junior Signalman's Wing of 11 Signal Regiment before they were handed over to the Junior Infantry Battalion in the 1980s.

Ron Haslam ventured to Ouston in 1979 and virtually cleaned up on his various Pharaoh Yamahas. (Mortons Archive)

After an absence of ten years, in May 1979 the Northumberland Sidecar Association arranged a national motorcycle event with many star names present. With a large crowd in attendance, Ron Haslam swept the board with wins on his 250 cc, 350 cc and 750 cc Pharaoh Yamahas before handing some of his £1,000 winnings back to the proposed Phil Haslam Memorial Races which were scheduled to be run at Ouston later that year.

Only Scotsman Ronnie Mann got the better of Haslam that day when he pipped him in the 125 cc race while Terry Haslam and Bonner Freeman won the sidecar final and the £500 prize money that went with it. Other names that featured that day were TT ace Joey Dunlop, Steve Tonkin, Dave Dean and Bill Simpson before hail showers halted proceedings.

The track remained a staple of the northern club racing scene throughout the 1980s, with the North East Motor Cycle Racing Club mainly holding meetings, which proved popular with a number of Scottish riders who could just hop over the border, but by the end of the decade racing had ceased.

A military presence continued at Ouston with the 39 Regiment Royal Artillery on the site from 1995 to 2015. Nowadays, the runways are used by Northumbria Police for driver training and as a stop-off point for nuclear warheads convoys en route via road between RNAD Coulport and AWE Aldermaston as part of the UK Trident programme.

The field barrels down one of the runway straights at a meeting at Ouston in the mid-1960s. (Terry Wright)

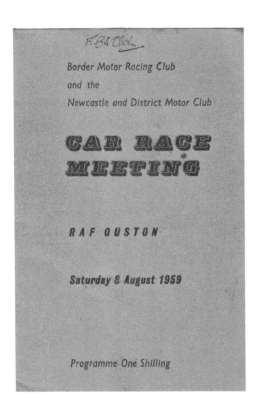

Border Motor Racing Club
and the
Newcastle and District Motor Club

CAR RACE MEETING

RAF OUSTON

Saturday 8 August 1959

Programme One Shilling

Left: A car race programme cover from 1959 at RAF Ouston signed by Jim Clark. (Terry Wright)

Below: Now deserted and devoid of motor race action, the overgrown runways of Albemarle Barracks, which once hosted top-class events. (Cartersport)

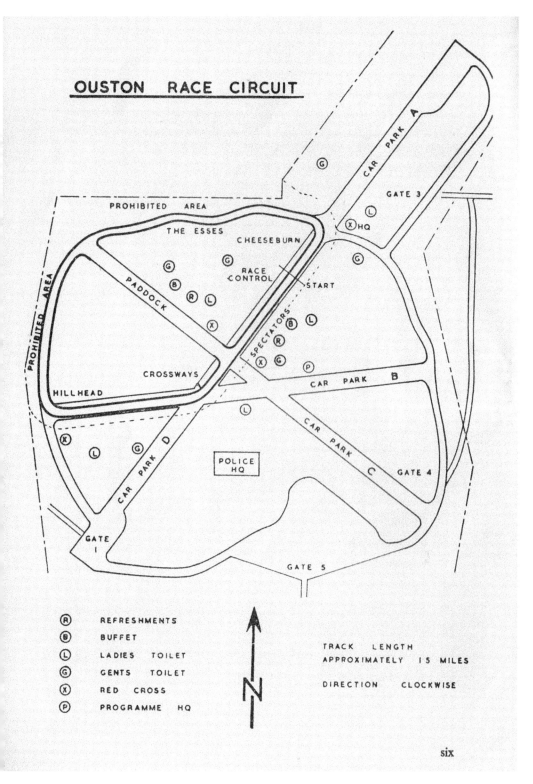

The track layout at Ouston, which remained very similar over the years. (Terry Wright)

DARLINGTON & DISTRICT MOTOR CLUB: THE PIONEERS

Darlington and District Motor Club are one of Britain's longest-established motoring organisations, whose roots can be traced back to the start of the twentieth century. They started out not long after the invention of the motor car as Darlington and Bishop Auckland Motoring Club in 1905, but it wasn't until 1927 that they commenced organising motorsport events, which included grass track racing at Croft.

The club and its activities lapsed during the First World War, but after hostilities ceased it reformed as Darlington Motor Club before, in 1920, it amalgamated with the newly formed Motor Cycle Club and South End Motor Club, which led to a unique concept of running bikes and cars at the same meetings, which has continued to this day.

The association with Croft continued into the early 1930s before a move to Willow Bridge near Barton saw grass track racing resume, but it wasn't long before the Second World War forced the cessation of activities again.

In 1946, the club emerged as Darlington and District Motor Club (D&DMC), and such was the enthusiasm of members that the first post-war event was run before petrol was allowed for pleasure purposes, so they organised a grass track for pedal cycles. However, by 1948 things had improved sufficiently to allow the promotion of motor race events around the newly available Croft Airfield, and for the next couple of years the club continued to put on race meetings.

Such was the recognition of the club's commitment to the sport in those tentative post-war years that the club's badge is proudly displayed in the Daytona Museum of Speed in Florida.

D&DMC's association with Croft continued until 1958 when the Air Ministry put an end to it being used for racing purposes meaning the club had to look for alternative venues. Airfields at Thornaby and Catterick were seconded and along with a highly successful Hill Climb at Catterick and as custodians of the Scott Trial the club continued to flourish.

In the 1960s, the reopening of Croft saw D&DMC continue to organise meetings through the 1970s, including televised rallycross and the burgeoning Battle of Britain Trophy meetings, which traditionally took place on the August bank holiday Monday and attracted huge crowds to see star guests who were contracted to appear by their personal sponsors and who were presumably paid handsomely for their attendance.

Then in the 1980s, D&DMC were at the forefront of the rallycross revolution when Croft reopened in 1982 and for over two decades were responsible for organising and running the major rallycross events including the InterNations Cup, Rallycross Superprix and MSA British Rallycross Grands Prix.

The club celebrated its centenary in 2005 and nowadays boasts a healthy membership incorporating motorcycle trials riders, competitors in race, rally, sprints and rallycross, senior officials and around a hundred fully trained circuit marshals. D&DMC also organises and runs the extremely popular Northern Saloon and Sports Car Championship, which takes place at various circuits.

CROFT: THE EARLY DAYS

Croft (Aerodrome) was constructed in 1940 and opened in October 1941. It was originally intended as a satellite base to RAF Middleton St George (today better known as Teesside Airport) and its first squadron was 78 Sqn with Whitley bombers, from October 1941. 419 Sqn RCAF (Royal Canadian Air Force) arrived at the airfield a year later in October 1942, and various other squadrons occupied the North Yorkshire airfield throughout the Second World War.

At the end of hostilities Croft saw very little activity, apart from some training usage, and finally closed in the summer of 1946. The following year, businessman and councillor John Neasham acquired the lease to the land and formed the Darlington and District Aero Club. The club folded after only five years and subsequently the airfield fell into disuse.

It was still owned by the RAF, however, and in 1951 they changed the name of the airfield to Croft Airport, using it as a Relief Landing Ground. At the time the airfield was also occasionally being used for motor race meetings by Darlington and District Motor Club. On various layouts utilising the runways and perimeter roads as a circuit, they held races throughout the 1950s.

One of the first meetings took place in May 1951 for various classes of 'Solo Motor Cycles' and 'Three Wheelers'. It was the usual format of heats, finals, and handicap races with some pretty generous prize money on offer – £10 to the winner of each event. That equates to £338 in today's money and with prizes of £6 for second, £4 for third and £2 for fourth, as well as £2 for each heat winner, it was certainly worthwhile.

Leading the entry was TT and Manx Grand Prix winner Denis Parkinson from Wakefield on his 350 cc and 500 cc Nortons as well as another former TT winner, Eric Houseley from Chesterfield (347 cc Matchless and 499 cc BSA). The vast majority of the 107 solo entrants (and only six sidecars) were from the North East and Yorkshire although V. R. Green (Birkenhead), A. J. Samuels (Manchester) and S. R. West (Oxford) had slightly longer journeys in those pre-motorway days.

There was also a comprehensive circuit map, which bears little resemblance to the track of the 1960s and 1970s, nor the latest version from 1995 onwards. The pits were roughly on the exit of the former Sunny Corner (now Sunny In and Out) and at the top end of the old Railway Straight. Cowton Corner appears to be around the location of the 'cut-through' on the run to the Jim Clark Esses before the track disappears through the no-longer-visible roads of Dalton Corner, Birch Curve and Birch Corner before starting to run back through Halnaby Corner, Bigland Curve and Walmire Turn, which would be in the vicinity of the residential houses now at Vince Moor East.

Various officials from Darlington & DMC at a very wet Croft in 1964. (Terry Wright)

The start of a reliability trial in the early 1900s organised by Darlington and Bishop Auckland Motoring Club. (Terry Wright)

Above: Darlington & DMC have had an involvement with Croft for over seventy-five years. Here is a saloon car race start from 1971. (Tony Todd)

Right: The programme cover from the Daily Mirror Trophy meeting from 1964, the year the circuit emerged as Croft Autodrome. (Terry Wright)

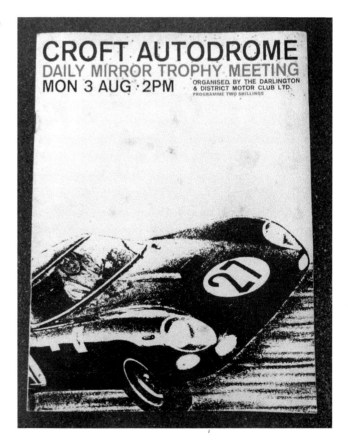

CROFT AUTODROME
DAILY MIRROR TROPHY MEETING
MON 3 AUG · 2PM

ORGANISED BY THE DARLINGTON
& DISTRICT MOTOR CLUB LTD.
PROGRAMME TWO SHILLINGS

From 1950 to 1990, Darlington & DMC were custodians of the Scott Trial, during which time the event was moved to Swaledale where it has remained since. (Tony Todd)

GRASS TRACK RACING: DISHING THE DIRT

After the end of the Second World War and despite rationing still being prevalent and the inevitable austerity, society was emerging, none more so than in motorsport and in particular, motorcycling.

Motor clubs were dusting off the cobwebs of years of inactivity, and competitors, many of whom had served during the war, wanted a slice of the action. Venues started to spring up, and back in those pre-health and safety executive and less environmentally conscious days, organising was a fairly simple process. Permission of the landowner was sought before applying to the local Auto Cycle Union (ACU) for a permit, send out regulations, advertise the event in the local and specialised press and away you went.

Northallerton and District Motor Club was one such organisation who were prevalent in the early 1950s and who organised mainly off-road events. Two such meetings were in the space of eight months of each other both in and around the town, namely a Grass Track in August 1952 followed by a Scramble in April 1953.

Grass Track racing was very popular in the region for many years and regularly saw some local Speedway aces take on other riders in the oval arena in four lap sprints of up to a dozen competitors. Also popular with spectators were the sidecars as they wrestled their way around the quarter mile course, usually in the opposite direction to the solos.

The meeting in 1952 took place at the Show Field in Northallerton 'by kind permission of Mr J. Almond'. Some questions fired in the direction of my ninety-year-old Aunt Jean (whom the programmes belong to and whose brother – No. 12 L. Wade – was racing that day) told me the track was in the vicinity of the Bluestone Ground at the rear of County Hall, just off Racecourse Lane. You know the playing fields you look over when waiting for a southbound train at Northallerton railway station.

The programme doesn't list the hometowns of the competitors, just their affiliated clubs, but as well as my uncle Les listed above, notable names from the time included the Tate brothers from the Swainby area, George Dawkins who ran the motorcycle shop in Bedale for many years and the Stead brothers from Northallerton. Middlesbrough speedway stalwart Frank Hodgson and Thirsk garage proprietor Jack Moss were others on the entry list.

Scrambling was different to grass track racing and usually held on hilly or rolling land and although the eastern fringes of Northallerton do have some undulations, the location of the event in 1953 at Hailstone Moor wasn't particularly conducive to either. Again, the exact location isn't defined but basic research would have the track at Bullamoor, somewhere between the top of Scholla Lane and Crosby Court. The club acknowledged the permission of Messrs L. Bramley, H. Hill, and O. Johnson, so presumably these were the landowners.

Familiar names from the previous year's aforementioned Grass Track were again in evidence, such as George Dawkins, Alf Stead, Maurice Tate, and Les Wade, while local ace Bert Hind along with Norman Crooks, later to become an established motorcycle dealer in Northallerton, and Ken Saddington from Great Broughton, were others entered at the meeting.

There is a reference to Eric H. Smithson, printer and stationer, Northallerton, on the Scramble programme while the back page of the Grass Track programme invites readers to a Saturday Night Trial later in the month, starting from Zetland Street at 10 p.m. – whatever that entailed! Sadly, no results are recorded for either meeting.

Grass track racing hasn't always been confined to two and three wheels as various disciplines of four-wheeled racing in farmers' fields have developed over the years. Disciplines such as Autocross were popular in the 1950s and 1960s, which consisted of a basic course laid out in a grass or stubble field whereby cars, either in groups or

Thirsk motorcycle dealer Dennis Teasdale, with passenger John Atkinson, was a leading light on the 1970s sidecar grass track scene. (Mortons Archive)

individually, were timed against the clock. Ostensibly, that morphed into rallycross on part-loose, part-sealed surfaces, but the two sports survive as individual entities in their own right with Causey Park near Morpeth still hosting Autograss meetings.

Another such variant was centred around stock car racing except instead of being located in a stadium and on shale, an oval circuit on grass was a cheaper alternative for all sorts of home-made specials to rock up under the auspices of banger racing.

One such venue was the domain of the Bellerby family at Mossa Grange near Northallerton who hosted a number of car grass track meetings in the 1970s. Prior to the development of the sport, which is now known as Autograss and sees many hundreds of competitors converge on venues up and down the country (including places locally in the past such as Lartington, Kiplin, Catterick, Tunstall and latterly Thornbrough near Masham), nowadays the cars are engineering masterpieces, although there are still classes for 'budget' racers.

Looking back to the sport's infancy, when there weren't such things as enclosed fuel cells, multi-point roll cages or flameproof suits, and quite often the contraptions were as if from a scene in the movie *Mad Max*, I wonder what today's health-and-safety-conscious world would make of such motorised anarchy.

Darlington's Ted Scott was another rider to establish himself in sidecar grass tracks. (Mortons Archive)

Chris Baybutt (500 Seiger), pictured here in 1977, along with brother Dave were very successful solo competitors regularly competing on local events. (Mortons Archive)

The early meetings of Autocross and Autograss were held at local venues, including Mossa Grange near Northallerton, including this one from 1975. (Tony Todd)

Safety wasn't a major priority with some home-built 'Specials' as demonstrated by this example from Mossa Grange in 1975. (Tony Todd)

CROFT CLOSES ITS DOORS: THE END - OR WAS IT?

All good things must come to an end, so the saying goes, and when landowner Bill Chaytor sounded the death knell for Croft Autodrome in 1981, it looked as if that was it for the North East's premier (and only) permanent racetrack.

Back in the mid-1960s when it became Croft Autodrome and Bruce Ropner's consortium heralded an exciting vision for the 1.75-mile track, there was a desire for such a facility. But some fifteen or so years later, despite one or two prestigious meetings and particularly the August bank holiday Battle of Britain meetings attracting huge crowds, interest had dwindled, and the circuit owners were faced with a decision.

The infrastructure and buildings, still based on post-war facilities, were starting to become dilapidated and the track, never the smoothest of surfaces, was in need of some repair. Dwindling crowds and an impending recession meant there wasn't the money there to spend on keeping Croft going, or perhaps there was and it just wasn't feasible to be spent on making the place more profitable at that time.

So, it was announced that at the end of the 1981 season the site would be returned to agricultural use and the asphalt straights, all three of them former runways, would be bulldozed as they were no longer needed. That final meeting, to be run by the British Racing and Sports Car Club (BRSCC) Northern Centre under the stewardship of Frank and Emily Wright, was scheduled to be held on 18 October but was put back a week much to the frustration of Croft's most successful driver, Andy Barton.

Barton had sixty-eight career wins around Croft and was planning to add to that tally, and such were the celebrations planned that he'd booked a holiday for the following week only to find that the date had shifted and he couldn't reschedule his plans. A Croft meeting without the venerable Geordie was like strawberries without cream, but alas the two-day meeting went ahead.

Such was the significance of the event that a capacity entry was received and a healthy crowd of both loyal locals and a few just along for the occasion were greeted by typical mixed weather as intermittent showers shared the stage with late autumnal sunshine as a relaxed practice and qualifying on Saturday paved the way for Sunday afternoon's magnificent seven races.

A leisurely start as ever on a Sunday at Croft due to local planning regulations that exist to this day meant no action until after the 12 noon curfew, but the first action on track saw John Booth clinch a thrilling fifteen-lap Bernard Hunter Crane Hire Formula Ford 1,600 race in his SHS Van Diemen ahead of local Darlington driver Wally Warwick. Warwick was out only for the third time in his Reynard and was in with a shout of the win before an excursion around the outside of the marshals' post at Tower Bend saw him settle for second ahead of Penrith farmer Tony Allinson (Van Diemen).

Next up was the Airmech Engineering Services/Audio Pro Hi-Fi Modsports Championship encounter over ten laps where Mark Hales and another Croft regular Tony Sugden scrapped it out in an epic race-long duel. Hales had to up the lap record in his quest for success in his 3.0-litre V6 Bedstor Marcos Ford GT as he got the better of Sugden's AET Esprit, which wouldn't be classified as it wasn't eligible for the championship due to running a non-turbocharged FVC engine.

The third race of the day saw competitors line up in the Harrison Brothers Steeplejacks Northern FF2000 Championship race with Croft debutante Russell Spence taking the victory in his Euroroof Royale-Nelson. Having only seen the track for the first time during Saturday's qualifying, the young Bradford driver set a new lap record for good measure as he finished ahead of Dave Sutherland's Neil Brown Royale RP30.

An eclectic mix of cars and drivers had assembled for the BRSCC Northern Special Saloon Championship race including George 'Welly' Potter's space-aged Esprit Chevrolet which shot off the line leaving the opposition in its wake. Middlesbrough's Jeff Wilson set about chasing it down in his equally awesome 5.0-litre Chevvy-engined Beetle and eventually saw the chequered flag ahead of Phil Barak in the ex-Gerry Marshall V8 'Baby Bertha' Vauxhall Firenza Chevrolet. A notable fourth place went to the ageing Chevrolet Camaro of Richmond driver Brian Morris, who in later years would go on to manage the new Croft Circuit.

Race five featured the BRSCC Formula Libre contingent, sadly without Barton, but the Newburn-based team still managed to get the victory in the hands of Phil Bennett whose Formula Atlantic-specification March BDA 792 saw off Vin Malkie's Chevron after fancied runner Jim Evans had wrecked his LEC Shadow at the infamous chicane in practice.

Following a parachute display by the Fewster Woodkirk Fireflies, a little nostalgia was the order of the day for the penultimate race as competitors lined up for the Historic Handicap for cars from 1930 to 1965. While Mike Harrison took the win in the Brabham BT2, all eyes were on Croft boss Bruce Ropner in a Sunbeam Talbot who was up against fellow shareholder Keith Schellenberg's mighty 4.4-litre Bentley for runner-up spot. Ropner got the better of his business partner but typically forfeited his award.

So, on to the final race, which was a consolation race for the non-qualifiers in the earlier FF1600 race along with certain invited drivers, one of which was Wally Warwick who crossed the line to take the last ever chequered flag, and by doing so won the Skippers Ford Trucks trophy for his endeavours. But there was a final piece of silverware to be awarded and that went to Dick Vaughan, in his first ever race, who finished last in the last ever race, and who was presented with a commemorative plate by Messrs Ropner and Schellenberg.

One final act came from Mick Mills who demolished the much-maligned Chicane for a final time leaving the wreckage to be collected by souvenir hunters while in the clubhouse they drank the place dry in tribute to the final show at the Yorkshire theatre of speed.

Only it wasn't, and within a year Croft was reverberating to the sound of racing cars again. But that's another story for another time...

Middlesbrough driver Jeff Wilson negotiates the Croft Chicane at the final meeting in October 1981. (Tony Todd)

George 'Welly' Potter puts his Esprit Chevrolet through its paces. (Tony Todd)

The programme cover for the final race meeting at Croft Autodrome in October 1981. (Terry Wright)

Scotsman Jim Crawford set the outright lap record at Croft in 1981, which will remain in the history books forever. (Tony Todd)

The mighty Special Saloons, once a regular sight at Croft, dwarf the formidable Chicane for one last time. (Tony Todd)

ACKNOWLEDGEMENTS

The author would like to thank the following people/organisations for permission to use copyright material in this book:

Tony Todd (www.tonytodd.photography)
Nick Nicholls at Mortons Archive
Spencer Oliver at Mortons Archive
Jane Skayman (Mortons Archive)
Terry and Yvonne Wright
Darlington and District Motor Club
Neil Sturgeon
Neil Pinkney
Andy Ellis
Andy and Pat Barton
Andy Barton Junior
Miss Jean Wade
Various programme publishers

Every attempt has been made to seek permission for copyright material used in this book. However, if we have inadvertently used copyright material without permission/acknowledgement we apologise and we will make the necessary correction at the first opportunity.

This book would not have been possible without the help from many kind and knowledgeable people who have gladly volunteered assistance when called upon.

Firstly, the main photographic source being my good friend Tony Todd whose wonderful archive has been a massive part of this project and I'm grateful for his unstinting help and support. This book wouldn't have been possible without his contributions.

Fellow lifelong motorsport enthusiasts Terry Wright and his wife Yvonne, who as members of Darlington and District Motor Club have been a wonderful mine of information and supplied pictures also. I'm grateful to you both.

The fantastic Mortons Archive, and in particular Jane Skayman, who have happily supplied a number of rare images for inclusion within these pages, many of which have never been published before. We go back a long way, and I knew I could count on them making a special book even better.

Mike Redfern, Michael Thompson, Steve 'Zak' Harland, Warren Taylor, Neil Pinkney, Andy Ellis, and Neil Sturgeon have all contributed in some way and a special thanks to my fellow rally driver and proof-reader Ashleigh Morris for ensuring the copy is fit to read.

Thanks to Croft Circuit Manager Tracey Morley and her staff along with BARC for their support too, and all previous managers, owners, officials, and competitors at Croft which features so prominently in this book.

A special acknowledgement goes to Hannah Chapman of the Darlington and Stockton Times whose encouragement for me to contribute a few trips down the motor-sporting memory lane during the difficult period of lockdowns, which she kindly published, led to this idea to do something more substantial.

Let's not forget Auntie Jean, whose collection of old programmes and press cuttings have been instrumental in jogging memories. I owe her (and Uncle Les) a deep debt of gratitude for ferrying me to events in my childhood that started my love affair with motorsport, which I harbour to this day.

And because there have been so many people who I have run ideas past and asked for help, invariably I'll forget someone, so if that person is you, I sincerely apologise.

Without my wife Sue there would be no book and, having put up with me for nearly forty years, this is dedicated to her for all her help and unstinting support for everything I do and have done.

Finally, a special thanks to Andy Barton, one of my childhood heroes, for agreeing to write the foreword. I never thought as a kid watching him race his various charges around Croft that one day I'd be writing this acknowledgement. It just goes to show that if you dream big enough, you can achieve the impossible.